C000128714

A HISTORY OF
LITTLEBOROUGH
PUBS

A HISTORY OF
LITTLEBOROUGH
PUBS

LITTLEBOROUGH HISTORICAL & ARCHAEOLOGICAL SOCIETY

TEMPUS

Dedicated to the memory of Alan Luke BSc, GIMA,
(1946-1992); founder member and chairman of Littleborough Historical
& Archaeological Society; good customer of several of the drinking
establishments mentioned in this book.

First published 2006

Tempus Publishing Limited
The Mill, Brimscombe Port,
Stroud, Gloucestershire, GL5 2QG
www.tempus-publishing.com

© Littleborough Historical and Archaeological Society, 2006

The right of Littleborough Historical and Archaeological Society
to be identified as the Author of this work has been asserted in
accordance with the Copyrights, Designs and Patents Act 1988.

All rights reserved. No part of this book may be reprinted
or reproduced or utilised in any form or by any electronic,
mechanical or other means, now known or hereafter invented,
including photocopying and recording, or in any information
storage or retrieval system, without the permission in writing
from the Publishers.

British Library Cataloguing in Publication Data.
A catalogue record for this book is available from the British Library.

ISBN 0 7524 4131 0

Typesetting and origination by Tempus Publishing Limited.
Printed in Great Britain.

CONTENTS

ACKNOWLEDGEMENTS

It fell to me as Alan Luke's nephew and a member of the society to co-ordinate the new research and documentation of additional material which has enabled the society to produce this second edition.

I have been ably assisted by Harold and Caroline Bamber, Peter Cryer, Graham Pearson and Jackie Ryder in this task and thank them for the research, photography, typing and proof reading that they have undertaken in giving that assistance.

I would also like to point out that in a work of this nature there are bound to be some omissions and errors; we would like to hear of any corrections. The Bambers have asked me to point out that the handwriting of the recorder of licensing information at the magistrate's court in the 1980s and 1990s has resulted in having to guess the spelling of some licensees' names.

Mark Pearson
Littleborough, June 2006

INTRODUCTION

In 1983, Alan Luke, then chairman and a founder member of the society, produced a book entitled *A History of Littleborough Pubs*, which ran to fifty-six pages and which he published privately. The print run was 400 and it soon sold out. After a period of twenty-three years, and following several requests from society members, book sellers and licensees, we have undertaken to revise and update the book for a much larger and expanded second edition.

To paraphrase the *Lincoln Da Vinci Code Pub Tour*, this book is a history of Littleborough 'pubs, both existing and those that have disappeared into the alcoholic haze of time'.

The basic research for this book was completed by Alan Luke in the early 1980s. However, over the last twenty-odd years, more records have come to light which complete, amplify and, in some cases, contradict the original research material.

Using Alan Luke's work as a basis, we have grown the book into 128 pages, included more photographs and document illustrations and corrected the errors that came to light after the original publication. We hope that this new edition will appeal to all those who bought his original book as well as those who were unable to obtain a copy.

The preface to the first edition was simply entitled 'Early History and General Records'. We have left this introduction fairly intact, as it serves as a general introduction to local beer brewing and selling.

This is not the end of research into the history of Littleborough pubs. There are three public houses mentioned in this book for which a location has yet to be found. Alan Luke identified the first – the Golden Fleece. We have found two more – the Two Foot public house and the Royal Oak at Dearnley. All three may be identified by further research into census information now more widely available through the Internet as a result of digitisation projects undertaken by the Public Record Office.

Associations between pubs and landlords would benefit from further study. For instance, there is little doubt that Hamer Hollinrake was licensee of the Blue Ball at Smithy Bridge from 1900 to 1905 before moving to the Railway Hotel in that year, remaining there until 1906 when he then took over the tenure of the Caldermoor, a pub where he remained landlord until 1917 when he moved to the Red Lion. His is an easy name to spot and track the movement of, within the records that are available. But what of other landlords with more common names?

The licensing laws which came into force in the early 1870s required local licensing authorities to keep better records of the inns, hotels, public houses and beerhouses lying within their jurisdiction. In the latter years of the nineteenth century and early years of the twentieth century, much pressure was put upon these authorities to reduce the number of licensed premises and rid their locality of beerhouses, much regarded as unsanitary breeding grounds for criminal activity, drunkenness and loutish behaviour. But what of the years before 1872? Research then relies upon census returns, trades directories, reports of (usually) criminal activity connected with, or inquests held at, such establishments, published in local newspapers. During the last twenty-three years, we have been able to add to the lists of licensees for pubs as a result of research using these sources of information – but there are still gaps in this information, yet to be resolved.

So, as with any work of historical research, we do not pretend that this is a definitive history; it remains simply a more complete history. The society hopes that by publishing a second edition, memories of past hostelries will be stirred, photographs pulled out of old boxes, drawers and albums and other memorabilia relating to the retailing of alcohol in the locality will surface. The society would be pleased to be offered the opportunity of copying and/or preserving such memorabilia for the future.

EARLY HISTORY
AND GENERAL RECORDS

It is without doubt that the earliest records of beer brewing and selling in the district are now lost, along with the associated artefacts such as the old copper brew pans and beer warmers. Many families may still keep a few mementoes of the old utensils; we have seen an old cone-shaped vessel that was used to warm beer on cold winter nights and the warmth it gave was no doubt most welcome. However, the description of these items and the techniques of brewing are beyond the aim of this book. We are merely concerned with the records that are available to us and will touch on the more material aspects when the need arises.

The earliest records of brewing and selling that we have been able to find involve the fines meted out at the early Rochdale Manor Courts. The following are examples of these:

> 1335   The wife of Nicholas the smith, for licence to brew; iijd.
> The wives of Thomas de Hall, Geoffrey of the Hill and Adam de Paris each fined iijd for bad beer brewed.

> 1336   William Ffox for selling ale against the Assize, vjd.
> Magota de Paris for brewing ale against the Assize, surety Nicholas de Clegg iijd.

Each of these illustrates that from an early date beer was much used as a source of taxation. Indeed it is likely that these Assizes date back to the time when much of the area was owned by Whalley Abbey, for we find in the re-published book by Ammon Wrigley, *Annals of Saddleworth*:

> 1291   The Abbot of Cockersand claimed amendments of Assize of bread and beer broke in Quick (Saddleworth)

> The monks were almost always after something good for the belly, and perhaps the Abbot thought that if he got a quart of Saddleworth's home brewed ale down his neck, it would make him believe he was Pope of Rome.

Perhaps a little biased, but illustrative of the reasons why, in modern times, a vast amount of income is derived from the tax on the humble pint of mild. By 1556, the cost of a licence to brew had risen considerably, for in that year, 'Annes Butterworth and James Matthewes sell Alle without Lyssens and are warned to leave off upon payne of 20s every of them'.

Durn, viewed towards Stephenson's railway viaduct; Ealees Hall was probably on the right-hand side of Halifax Road as viewed, where the viaduct buttress now stands.

This last record brings us nearly to the time of our first mention of a Littleborough Inn, for in the 1626 Manor Survey we find John Butterworth in possession of, 'The moiety of a tenement called the Ealees wherein he now dwelleth being converted to an Inn, the site consisting of a little croft and garden'. We have not been able to place this inn exactly but we suspect it could have been in the area of the present Red Lion as it was stated to be close to Halifax Road.

Throughout the ages inns have been meeting places of men of business. It is inside the portals of these houses that many decisions affecting the life of Littleborough have been made. The early Turnpike Acts often refer to inns as meeting places for the trustees. In 1760 for example, the Todmorden to Littleborough Trust met on four occasions at the sign of the Red Lion, the house of Mary Gibson. In the minutes of the same trust we find this mention for the year 1798, 'An allowance of ale for workmen repairing the road at Deanhead.'

The ale allowance is met in all aspects of early records. We have seen parish church records of similar allowances. This practice continued into the early years of the last century for Mr Harold Tate, Parkhill House, recalled that when, around 1910, Cleggs of Shore Mill worked weekends they sent for a beer allowance which they were allowed to have for 'three ha'pence a pint instead of the usual tuppence'.

In these early years, Littleborough was a mainly rural area depending on sheep farming and associated handloom weaving; it was not until the middle of the nineteenth century that the effects of the Industrial Revolution were felt, giving rise to the town population and a need for more public houses.

Prior to 1830, it was a requirement of all inns and taverns that they provided accommodation and stabling in addition to refreshment. The majority of these inns were, by necessity, larger buildings most likely situated by the side of thoroughfares. In Littleborough, these early inns, such as the Falcon and

Littleborough, from Blackstone Edge.

the Rake, served both the rural and passing population, and it was not until the Beerhouse Act of 1830 was passed that a vast increase in the number of drinking establishments was made possible.

The Beerhouse Act was an effort by Parliament to allow for the provision of beer to the growing urban population. This Act of Parliament allowed any householder who could meet the very basic conditions imposed by the Act, to turn his house into a beerhouse. As the industrial population grew, so did these mainly unchecked establishments. The 1860s and 1870s saw an explosion in the number of such beerhouses in Littleborough and it was this period that provided us with the many pub names that disappeared earlier in the last century. The following list of beer retailers appears in the 1873 directory, all except one without a 'pub name'; an interesting exercise is to give 'locals' to these people. We have been able to place twelve with some certainty.

1873 DIRECTORY

John Alletson	Hare Hill
Jonathon Arm	Blackstone Edge Road
John Ashworth	Summit
Samuel Baker	Featherstall
Robert Brearley	Featherstall
William Carter	Church Street
Robert Fletcher	Whitelees
Enoch Gibson	Three Lane Ends
James Greenwood	Rock Nook

Sally Hollows	Ealees
Peter Ormerod	Summit
Henry Rogers	Smithy Nook
Thomas Stott	Sladen
Hush Tate	Lower Shore
William Whipp	Hollingworth Lake
Thomas Wild	Cleggswood Lane
Thomas Wild	Church Street
John Woods	Star Hotel, Hollingworth

The trades directories give many references to the beer sellers of Littleborough but it is not always possible to allocate an individual pub to them. It appears that some of them may only have had an off-licence; the first mention in the directories that referred to an 'Out Door Licence' was in the 1885, for Ann Smith of Shore.

By the start of the 1870s, it was recognised that something was needed to curb the growing number of unregulated, sometimes unsanitary and often crime-ridden beerhouses. In 1872, an Act of Parliament transferred the power of licensing control from the excise to the local authorities. Local authorities were given the power to refuse licence renewals and prevent new beerhouses from opening.

With the 1872 Act came a standardisation of recording licensing information and the records from 1872 onwards, which are now lodged with the Magistrates Courts, are more accurate and complete.

Unfortunately, the 1872 Act which gave the power of refusal of licence to the local authorities also gave the power of impoverishment, as a licence refused could have led to the loss of income for the beerhouse keeper in an age where income support was unheard of. As a result, local authorities were minded not to close a beerhouse if it would have resulted in the owner and his family transferring to the local workhouse.

Lower Shore.

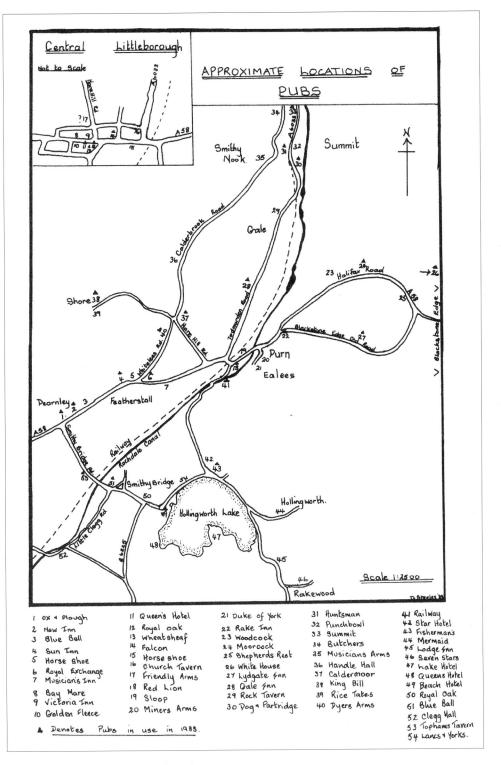

Location map taken from the first edition.

This situation was remedied in 1904 with the enactment of the Compensation Act. This Act of Parliament allowed local authorities to compensate the owners of beerhouses that were closed down. From that date, local authorities could set about the systematic closure of those beerhouses which had attracted too much attention from the local constabulary.

In a report of licensing hearings given in the *Rochdale Observer* of 9 February 1907, regarding the closure of beerhouses, it was stated that: 'According to the returns supplied by the police there are 214 persons to every licensed house in Littleborough, 235 in Milnrow, 260 in Norden, 221 in Wardle and 290 in Whitworth.'

In the following history of pubs we do not intend to dwell on the distinction between hotels or public houses with full licences, and beerhouses, but some idea of this distinction may be gained from a look at this list of 1907, which gives twenty-eight with licence and thirteen beerhouses.

FULL LICENCE		BEERHOUSES
Beach Hotel	Moorcock	Bay Mare
Blue Ball	Mermaid	Dog & Partridge
Blue Bell	New Inn	Duke of York
Coach & Horses	Queen Anne	Dyers Arms
Dog & Partridge	Queens (L'boro)	Horse Shoe (L'boro)
Falcon	Railway (L'boro)	Musicians
Fishermans	Railway (Sm. Br.)	Parkhill House
Gale	Rake	Punch Bowl
Gate	Red Lion	Queens (Holl. Lake)
Horse Shoe (Featherstall)	Royal Oak (L'boro)	Rock Tavern
King William	Royal Oak (Sm. Br.)	Shepherds Tavern
Lake Hotel	Summit	Victoria
Lancashire & Yorkshire	Sun	Woodcock
Lodge	Wheat Sheaf	

The two main associations involved with beer sellers at this time were the Rochdale & District Licensed Victualler's Association and Rochdale & District Off Licence Holders Protection Association. The latter was established in 1894 and the former dates back to at least 1879.

The number of breweries involved in this area has now been reduced to the major companies such as Tetley Walker and Bass Charrington. Some of the original brewers like Massey, Ramsdens and Phoenix having either gone out of business or been taken over by the larger combines. The only Littleborough breweries we have been able to trace are the Littleborough Brewery Co., based at the Wheat Sheaf, and the Dearnley Brewery Co. based at Greengate. This latter company was owned in 1853 by J.J.H. Ormerod and in 1892 by R.L. Watson when the *Rochdale Observer* announced its failure. Many of the early beerhouses would have brewed their own ale. We have been unable to discover when this practice died out.

The main part of this book consists of individual pub histories in alphabetical order. The list of landlords for each pub is as accurate as far as we are able to ascertain and is based mainly on the Licensing Records and Trades Directories, with individual references from a variety of books and papers.

On the previous page is reproduced a map which appeared in the first edition of this book. Drawn by Di Steeles, a former member of the society, it illustrates the location of all of the known inns, public houses and beerhouses in Littleborough and hopefully acts as a guide to locate some of the more obscure of these properties.

LITTLEBOROUGH PUBS
AN A TO Z

BAY MARE

Research in the archive editions of the *Rochdale Observer* and the *Rochdale Times* reveal that it was in 1870 that Isaac Alletson first applied for a full licence for his establishment, the Bay Mare public house, situated at No. 90 Church Street. This would suggest that the Bay Mare was a public house rather than a beerhouse, as previously thought. This is further reinforced by an article in the *Rochdale Times* of 16 January 1885, reporting the death of Isaac Alletson two days earlier and describing him as landlord of the Bay Mare public house, Church Street.

The first record of a landlord, however, is 1861 when the *Rochdale Observer* gave notice of an auction held in December that year at the Dog & Partridge, Caldermoor of, 'That Inn or Public House situated at Will Hill and known as the Bay Mare with yards and outbuildings in the occupation of George Rigg.' The 1881 census records:

> *Bay Mare Hotel, Church Street*
> Isaac Alletson; head; licensed victualler; aged 40; born Littleborough
> Elizabeth Alletson; wife; aged 42; born Littleborough
> Sarah Alletson; daughter; aged 19; unmarried; born Littleborough
> Mary Alletson; daughter; aged 11; unmarried; born Littleborough

The 1890 trade directory listed an Elizabeth Alletson, describing herself as 'beerseller'. This suggests that she may have been widowed in the nine years following the census.

We know that Alice Richards was the last landlady of this drinking establishment. The *Rochdale Times* on 27 January 1912 published details of the licence transfer to Alice Kershaw as sole executor of Samuel Kershaw and subsequent research may confirm that Alice Kershaw remarried and remained as landlady.

It is understood that the original beer engines could be seen in the cellar as late as the mid-1980s. Beer engines were often locally made and there is a record of a Mr Thomas Hanson of High Street, Rochdale, advertising himself as a Beer Engine Maker as far back as 1824.

The building still retains its connection with the trade by being a modern off-licence.

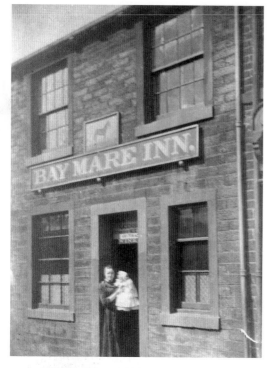 

Above left: Bay Mare public house, Church Street.

Above right: The Bay Mare as it stands today, maintaining its connection with the trade.

LIST OF LICENSEES:

1861	George Rigg	1892–1911	Samuel Kershaw
1870–1885	Isaac Alletson	1911–1914	Alice Kershaw
1885–1892	Elizabeth Alletson	1914–1915	Alice Richards
1892	Sarah Stott Kershaw		

BLACK SLOVEN

This is one of the early names for the public house at Clegg Hall. It is a public house with an interesting origin to its name, as can be seen from a note found in the 1935 edition of the *Littleborough Shopping Guide*:

Charles Turner, resided at Clegg Hall in the eighteenth century. He was a lover of the chase and owned a famous hunter named 'Black Sloven'. A Yorkshire sportsman was given the opportunity of trying the capabilities of Black Sloven. This was on the day that the Pike House Hounds were chasing a hare from Wardle. As soon as the Horse heard the 'sweet swelling' notes of the horn and the cry of 'Tally Ho', she went off like a shot and thro' the fields, over walls, over a coal pit windlass, not stopping until she had travelled several miles into Yorkshire. Although he managed to stay on, the rider vowed never again to trust his weight on the famous huntress. Mr Charles Turner died on the 2nd January 1773; Black Sloven walked in his funeral cortege bearing her master's hunting apparel.

This is an interesting tale that no doubt gave cause for another name to this pub - that of the Hare & Hounds. See the list of licensees under Clegg Hall for both these names.

BEACH HOTEL

This first appears in the directories of 1873 but earlier references can be found; for example the *Annals of Rochdale* tell us that £210 was stolen from Sladen's Beach Hotel in 1868 and the *Rochdale Observer* for May 1856 holds the following advertisement:

Hollingworth Lake
Pleasure Boats &c. James Sladen begs to intimate to the inhabitants of Rochdale and the surrounding neighbourhood that he has purchased a swift pleasure steamer and additional small swift paddle boats, which are now afloat on the above lake, every day and on Sunday evenings.

This Sunday evening trade caused quite a stir in the correspondence columns of the *Rochdale Observer*, being considered by some as a desecration of the Lord's Day. The boats did however weather the storm and have plied, on and off, for over 120 years.

In 1875 a skating rink was opened by Sladen and in 1880 the hotel was valued as follows, in a rating list: 'Uriah Sladen; Beach Hotel; Stables; Gigg Shed; Dancing Stage; Rental value £100.'

The Sladens were amongst those instrumental in bringing the popularity of Hollingworth Lake to the fore in the 1860s as a local resort.

In 1868, it is recorded that a Mr J. Wearden, late pointsman with the Lancashire & Yorkshire Railway Co. and now champion two-wooden-legged walker, gave entertainment in July of that year at the Beach Hotel. He walked one-quarter-of-a-mile in three minutes. Given his former occupation in connection with the railway, it would not be unreasonable to assume that his current predicament *viz.* two wooden legs may have had something to do with his former position as pointsman?

The hotel suffered a disastrous fire in 1901 and the present building retains the basic appearance of the restored hotel, which is now modernised and when it became 'Millers' earlier this century, the brickwork exterior was painted.

Research in the archive editions of the *Rochdale Observer*, *Rochdale Times* and *Rochdale Star* provide many references to this popular lakeside drinking establishment. Most notable are reports of the death of James Sladen on 31 August 1876 and claims against his estate in probate, and reports in the *Rochdale Star* and *Rochdale Times* of an ownership dispute in May 1889 between a Mr Starkie and a Mr Roberts, resulting in the closure of the house by the police. By the close of 1889 the building had been put up for auction. The *Rochdale Times* of 22 February 1890 includes a notice of that auction, thus:

To be sold by auction by Messrs. William, Swift and Oddy at the White Swan Inn, Yorkshire Street, Rochdale on Monday next, the 24th February 1890, at six for seven p.m., prompt, subject to Conditions of Sale to be then produced, all that Hotel or Public House, fully licensed known as the 'Beach Hotel', with the Tea Rooms, Dancing Stage, Skating Rink, Stabling and appurtenances thereto belonging, situate at Hollingworth Lake, near Rochdale.

Above left: Advertisement for James Sladen's Beach Hotel.

Above right: A later advertisement for the Beach Hotel.

The site contains an area of 5,137 square yards, and is held for the residue of two terms of 999 years and 999 years, created by Indentures of Lease dated respectively 1st July 1862 and 30th December 1869. The premises are sold subject to payment of the yearly rents amounting to £23 9s 4½d, reserved by and to the observance and performance of the respective lessee's covenants and the conditions contained in the respective Indentures of Lease. They are also sold subject to two further yearly charges of £5 and £2 respectively. The total of the annual charges affecting the premises is £30 9s 4½d.

The property is situated on the borders of Hollingworth Lake, and is the chief hotel at this favourite pleasure resort. The premises are in good repair and completely fitted with trade fixtures for conducting an extensive business. The purchaser can have actual possession on completion of his purchase.

The pub sold on that occasion for £1,400. It was auctioned again in 1907, when it made £2,500, according to a report in the *Rochdale Times* for 19 January of that year.

On 25 January 1908, the *Rochdale Times* gives a full report of the Littleborough Urban District Council's claims against the then landlord, John Whittaker, for his costs of the making up and sewering of Lake Bank; but by 19 January 1909, John Whittaker had entered into a deed of assignment/ arrangement with his creditors according to the *Rochdale Observer* published on that day.

The Beach Hotel following rebuilding in the early 1900s.

Renamed 'Millers', a contemporary view of this old establishment.

LIST OF LICENSEES:

1856-1876	James Sladen	1985-1988	Michael Brown
1876-1889	Uriah Sladen	1988-1989	Joseph Henry Pierce
1890-1902	Charles Rogers	1989-1991	Christopher Hewitt
1902-1909	John Whittaker	1991-1993	James Patterson
1909-1910	Norris Williamson	1993-1994	Anthony Lawrence White
1910-1917	Richard Barnes	1994	Sarah J. Ridgeway
1917-1919	Ann Barnes	1994-1995	Terrance Alan Hargood
1919-1924	Edmund Lord Barnes	1995	Gloria Ann Shackleton
1924-1926	Nathaniel Taylor	1995-1996	Wayne Reynolds
1926-1927	Thomas Taylor Roberts	1996-1997	John Kidby
1927-1928	David Holt	1997	Mark James Hadfield
1928-1930	Nathaniel Taylor	1997-1998	George McAleny
1930-1937	Leo Harwood	1998	Robin Larner
1937-1951	Poss. Leo Harwood	1998	Alan Hibbert
1951-1953	Ellen Winnifred Harwood	1998-1999	Jason James Hayes
1953-1973	Herbert Collins	1999-2000	Terrance Alan Hargood
1973-1977	James Douglas Almond	2000-2003	Vincent Gerald Miller
1977-1984	Joseph Henry Pierce	2003-2005	Nicholas Paul Lumb
1984-1985	Daniel Jackson		

BLUE BALL

The present building that stands set back from Smithy Bridge Road was built in 1964. It replaced a building of complex internal features that had been built into the hillside at the edge of what was originally Walmsley Lane. The Old Blue Ball was unusual in that at one time the beer barrels were kept in the room of a cottage above and behind the bar rather than in the cellar below.

The earliest reference that we have been able to find is to a Mrs Holt, a victualler of Walms Lane, who lived here in 1818. The 1851 census tells us that James Collinge, Blue Ball, Walmsley Lane (he appears to have married the previous landlord's widow) helped his income from the inn by keeping on the trade of fulling miller. This double occupation was a feature of many landlords in the nineteenth century as can be seen in the notes on other pubs in this book.

In the archive editions of the *Rochdale Observer*, we find a report on 10 April 1869 of claims against the estate of the late James Fairburn who died on 10 October 1868. Later, on 28 August 1897 is advertising an auction of livestock at the Blue Ball on the instruction of Elizabeth Fairburn, his widow, 'who is leaving the country'.

In May 1869, it is reported that a new lodge of the Ancient Sons of Adam & Friendly Ploughman, a society founded in Bury in the 1930s was celebrated by a procession of about 200 people which started at the Blue Ball and finished at the Royal Oak in Littleborough.

The pub changed its name in 1970 (according to licensing records) to the Smithy Bridge.

LIST OF LICENSEES:

1818	Mrs Holt	1935-1958	Edwin Furner
1823	James Taylor	1958-1960	Fred Furner

The Blue Ball shortly before its demolition in 1964.

Contemporary view of the site of the Blue Ball.

1841	Sally Taylor	1960–1963	Philip Tennant
1848–1851	Robert Butterworth	1963–1970	Edwin Frank McCourt
1851–1852	James Collinge	1970–1978	Francis Gerald Green
1858–1861	Henry Bamford	1978–1980	Richard Wreggitt
1861–1869	James Fairburn	1980–1981	James Oliver Brown
1869–1872	James Fairburn (Jnr)	1981–1983	Herbert Turner
1872–1881	Elizabeth Fairburn	1983–1984	Ernest Burt
1885–1887	Edmund Ogden	1984–1991	Edward Lawton
1887–1897	Nanny Ogden	1991	Rodger Arthur Shepherd
1897–1900	Fielden Baron Crossley	1991–1994	Brian Albert Hutty
1900–1905	Hamer Hollinrake	1994	Peter Ronald Chorlton
1905–1909	William Crabtree	1994–1997	David Williams
1909–1920	Charles Butterworth	1997–2002	Yvonne Lillian Eastwood
1920–1935	Ada Butterworth	2002–2005	Andrea Maloney

BLUE BELL

Last licensed in 1956 the Blue Bell stood on the main road at Dearnley, next to the old Dearnley post office. It was demolished in 1974 and the Crowther Court flats stand on the site.

Photographs taken at the time of demolition show the building to have been a three-storeyed weaver's cottage with a full width of 'mullioned lights' on the upper floor and a loading bay on the middle floor. It was a substantial building and no doubt one of the reasons that it became a pub was to refresh the carters of woollen goods who would use this busy thoroughfare in the early nineteenth century.

The top storey of the building housed St Andrew's School which opened on 4 January 1869 in this building with forty pupils and Miss Emily Redfern as headmistress. They eventually transferred to a purpose-built school adjacent to Birch Hill Hospital.

The *Rochdale Observer* for 25 January 1873 contains an article describing a dinner given for the hands of Ralph Ashworth & Co. of Starring Pottery and lists William Butterworth as landlord. A report in the *Rochdale Times* from 30 October 1885 describes an auction of lands, cottages and a mill at Dearnley, held at the Blue Bell.

LIST OF LICENSEES:

1858	Thomas Berry	1911–1912	James Dawson
1872–1875	William Butterworth	1912–1917	Josiah Stoner
1875–1879	Charles Greenhalgh	1917–1927	John William Crossley
1879–1880	John Kershaw	1927–1933	Donald Powell Pullan
1880–1881	John Fielden	1933–1935	Martin Geoghegan
1881–1883	George Hoyle	1935–1936	Harry Carter
1883–1893	Charles Greenhalgh	1936–1945	George Dixon Carruthers
1893–1896	William Dugdale	1945–1947	Hannah Carruthers
1896–1899	William Daniels	1947–1949	Thomas Henry Lynch
1899–1900	Walter Taylor	1949–1952	William Joseph Clooney
1900–1901	John Robinson	1952–1953	Thomas Henry Lynch
1901–1904	William Dugdale	1953–1954	Joseph O'Hara
1904–1905	Albert Rowlinson	1954–1956	Alfred John Osbond Orr

Above: Site of the Blue Bell, Dearnley – now local authority housing.

Right: The Blue Bell, shortly before its demolition in 1974.

1905-1908	John Edward Rowell	1956	John Watson
1908-1910	Arthur Wilson	1956	William Melling
1910-1911	Frederick Ashworth	1956	Albert Smith
1911	John Dawson	1956-1958	Charles Admiral Keith

BUTCHERS, OR 'BULL AND BUTCHERS'

In the 1800 Turnpike Act mention is made of, 'A certain dwelling house now used as a public house situated at a place called Dog Hills in the division of Calderbrook'.

At this time it was in the occupation of Edmund Howard but by 1818 we have in occupation a James Lord, victualler and butcher, Dog Hills.

The history of this inn is directly connected with that of the Summit Inn, of which more, later. The inn was situated at the top of the lane (Wilmers Lane) that runs from the Summit Inn to Calderbrook Road, on the Summit side of the road; the foundations can still be seen.

LIST OF LICENSEES:

1800	Edmund Howard	1818	James Lord

CALDERMOOR

The following passage appears in Travis' notes on the *History of Littleborough*:

John Hurst of Caldermoor, when a young man, lived at a farm behind Wellington Lodge, and so became a playmate and intimate of the younger Newall lads. Afterwards he went to be a farmer's

Junction of Wilmers with Calderbrook Road, site of the Butchers Inn.

The Caldermoor public house.

man for a gentleman near Hollingworth, the old acquaintance still being continued, until by and by the Dog & Partridge Inn, Caldermoor, was about to become vacant, and John, who had arrived at manhood, and was courting a young woman, then residing at the Rake Inn, had the situation offered by his friends and so the matter was ended 'in the old way of an oft told tale'. He secured the cage and then fetched the bird.

The pub was built by Laurence and Sarah Newall in 1755. On the door lintel is a date stone of 1755, which refers to the building of the house by the Newalls who continued to own it until 1896. The name changed from the Dog & Partridge to the Caldermoor in November 1968.

A report in the *Rochdale Observer* of 14 March 1863 gives:

> The employees of Messrs H. & L. Newall were entertained at the house of Mr William Peacock, the Dog & Partridge Inn, Caldermoor, when about 200 sat down to a sumptuous repast. On the removal of the cloth the usual loyal toasts were given and a most agreeable evening was spent. The proceedings were diversified by singing, dancing & c.

We question how the pub was capable of hosting 200 workers for a meal, let alone provide them with the additional space required for dancing!

On 29 August 1868, the *Rochdale Observer* reported a notice of intention to form the New Benefit Building Society at the Dog & Partridge, with shares at £120 and half shares at £60. On 26 May 1883, the *Rochdale Observer* reported an auction of Moorfield House, Shore Road, held at the pub which saw the house sold to Dr McGill for £700. The 1881 census gives:

Caldermoor
William Peacock; head; farmer & innkeeper; aged 42; born Littleborough
Frances Peacock; wife; aged 30; born Littleborough
Tom Peacock; son; scholar; aged 10; born Littleborough
William H. Peacock; son; scholar; aged 7; born Littleborough
Charles Peacock; son; scholar; aged 5; born Littleborough
Elizabeth Peacock; daughter; scholar; aged 4; born Littleborough
Margaret Whittle; domestic servant; aged 19; unmarried; born Crewe
Ellen Sager; domestic servant; aged 17; unmarried; born Lancashire
Robert Crossley; farm servant; aged 18; unmarried; born Rochdale

The licensee remained in dual occupation until at least the 1890s, as the 1891 census records, Frances Peacock; head; widow; aged thirty-nine; innkeeper and farmer; born Healey, Lancashire.

We note that in the ten years between census returns, Frances has decided that she was not born in Littleborough.

Hamer Hollinrake, landlord, was summonsed in 1907 for serving after hours, according to a report in the *Rochdale Observer* from 9 March of that year. Hamer Hollinrake became landlord in 1906. Until that time, he had been landlord of the Blue Ball, Smithy Bridge.

LIST OF LICENSEES:

1818-1843	John Hurst	1940-1948	Ernest Challinor
1851-1861	Stephen Howard	1948-1952	George Holt
1861-1870	Ann Howard	1952-1954	Benjamin Ellis

1870–1890	William Peacock	1954–1957	Norman Vincent Christian
1890–1892	Frances Peacock	1957–1983	Duncan Robert Innes
1892–1896	George Greenhaugh	1983–1993	Steven Sarsfield
1896–1900	James Crabtree	1993	Alan Paul Hainley
1900	Hannah Crabtree	1993–1994	Karen J. Powles
1900–1906	John Crabtree	1994	Cathryn Ann Phillips
1906–1916	Hamer Hollinrake	1994–1997	Stuart Thomas Farley
1916–1927	Joseph Hollinrake	1997–1998	Clive Arthur Grayshaw
1927–1933	James Whatmough Parker	1998	Alan Cahill
1933–1935	Frank Blacka	1998–2002	Michael Peter Holmes
1935	Hannah Elizabeth Blacka	2002	Terence Bostock
1935–1938	William Heywood	2002–2005	Cheryl Reger
1938–1940	Vernon Norman Butler		

PRICE LIST

BEVERLEYS BEERS

APRIL 1965

DRAUGHT BEERS

	PER PINT	PER HALF-PINT
DARK MILD	1/7d.	9½d.
D.P.A.	1/8d.	10d.
TRINITY BITTER	1/10d.	11d.
MIDDLESBROUGH		
BITTER - -	2/-	1/-
OLD TOM - -	—	1/4½d.

BOTTLED BEERS

Imperial Pale Ale	1/6½d.	PER SMALL BOTTLE
Golden Eagle Ale	1/2½d.	do.
Beverleys Brown Ale	1/2½d.	do.
Beverleys Pale Ale	1/2½d.	do.
Old Warrior	1/2½d.	do.
Barley Wine	1/8½d.	PER NIP BOTTLE
Export Pale Ale	1/5d.	do.

Left: Price list from the Caldermoor, dated to 1962.

CHURCH TAVERN

We originally were only able to trace this tavern between the years 1843 and 1861. It is perhaps a case of giving a name to an off-licence as it appears in the directories under beersellers rather than inns and taverns. From the name one must assume that it was near the parish church and no doubt a detailed search of the census would locate it more accurately.

It appears that the landlord continued his occupation of the tavern until 1870 as the *Rochdale Observer* reported on 29 October 1870 an auction of brewing stock by the administrators of the late James Lee. It has been suggested that the Church Tavern stood on the site of what became the Horse Shoe public house on Church Street, of which more later, and certainly the dates would corroborate this suggestion, with the first recorded landlord of that establishment in 1872.

LIST OF LICENSEES:

1843 — 1870   James Lee

COACH & HORSES

Situated at the top of Blackstone Edge, this inn is now known as the White House. The last recorded occurrence of the name Coach & Horses was in December 1920 when the pub was officially changed to the White House, which is the pub that should be referenced for full details.

Photographs in the society collection indicate that the signpost, though often re-positioned, used to show a coach drawn by a number of horses. It is likely that the nineteenth-century sign has been destroyed, along with many others that would show the talents and skills of local signwriters.

We expand upon the references to the White House many years before the pub officially changed its name and refer readers to the White House for further details and a list of Licensees.

CLEGG HALL

As is mentioned in the introductory notes it is likely that as early as the fourteenth-century ale was being brewed in this locality.

It is not until the 1818 directory that we have mention of a landlord, at which time it had the name Hare and Hounds. The change of name can be seen in this list from the directories:

Above: Clegg Hall Hamlet, scene of perhaps the earliest brewing of beer recorded in the Littleborough area.

1818	Hare and Hounds
1837–1858	Black Sloven
1861	Hare and Hounds
1869	Licence taken away

In his book *Olden Days* the Revd G.R. Oakley tells us the story of the Clegg Hall boggart, the ghost is one of the early Cleggs from whom the name of the hall is taken:

It was in 1241 that the drawbridge was lowered at the fortress of the de Cleggs and the Baron rode off to fight in France with King Henry. He left behind his two sons Bertrand and Randulph under the care of his brother Richard who swore to 'guard them as the apple of mine eye'. One moonlight night, fourteen year old Bertrand was strolling in the grounds of the fortress when his uncle, in greed for the family fortunes, attacked him in the hope that his misdeed would go unnoticed. Thirteen-year-old Randulph witnessed the deed and with a cry of 'Brother Beware' warned of the attack. Richard, however, was well trained in the art of fighting and able to overpower both of the youths. He threw their bodies into the moat where they 'lay gleaming in the light of the moon'.

The Baron returned and, though nothing could be proved, banished his brother from the castle. Richard turned to his partner in crime at Stubley Hall and, with the aid of a secret passage from Stubley to Clegg, built in Saxon times, he returned at night to murder the Baron. The warning shout of 'Father, Beware!' was heard and the ghost of Randulph seen warning his father of impending doom. Richard was forced into the battlements from whence he fell to his death in the moat.

Randulph reappeared many times in later years to warn the de Cleggs of danger in times of battle.

Oakley's story was written in 1910, but three years earlier it is reported that bones had been found at Clegg Hall. It is not known whether these were of Randulph, Bertrand or Richard.

There is little evidence that the site of the present Clegg Hall was once occupied by a moated and fortified castle/fortress as the Revd Oakley suggested in 1910. Nor has any evidence of a tunnel linking the halls of Clegg and Stubley (situated on the A58 Featherstall Road) been discovered. The last landlord, John Milne, advertised:

John Milne; Hare & Hounds. This ancient and spacious hall offers refreshments – luncheons, dinners, teas; foreign and British spirits; home-brewed and Burton ales; draught and bottled porter; cigars etc. Strangers allowed to look through this ancient relic of the past.

LIST OF LICENSEES:

1818	Thomas Jones	1843–1845	Hannah Butterworth
1837	Robert Butterworth	1851	William Holt
1837	Thomas Hillingworth	1856–1861	John Milne

COLLIERS ARMS

This is the second Dearnley pub that we have met. It is now known as the New Inn, the name being changed in 1874. The colliery referred to is the Dearnley Colliery.

An interesting advertisement was placed in the *Rochdale Observer* of 4 October 1856, 'Look here, ye growers of bacon – you, too, the public. Mr Robert Buckley, Collier's Arms, Dearnley, near

Above and below: Clegg Hall in 2006, undergoing renovation to its former glory.

Littleborough, has a PIG that is now only 14 weeks old, and weighs the enormous weight of 105lbs.'

The name of the inn appears to have changed when extensive renovation, even rebuilding, took place in the 1870s. See New Inn for references and a list of licensees.

DOG & PARTRIDGE, CALDERMOOR

Originally known by this name, the inn is now known as the Caldermoor, under which the history notes and a list of licensees will be found.

DOG & PARTRIDGE, SUMMIT

In the year 1872 is the earliest record that we have been able to find for this public house. Situated as it is, close to the Fothergill & Harvey complex, it seems certain to have developed from a beerhouse that supplied the workers of the nineteenth-century. The 1881 census records:

Dog & Partridge Inn
Joshua Firth; head; beerseller; aged 52; born Todmorden
Sally Firth; wife; aged 53; born Walsden
Nathan Firth; son; maker-up at woollen mill; aged 23; unmarried; born Walsden
Tom S. Firth; son; clog iron maker; aged 22; unmarried; born Littleborough
Sam Firth; son; cotton weaver; aged 20; unmarried; born Littleborough
Clara Firth; daughter; cotton weaver; aged 16; unmarried; born Littleborough
Fanny A. Firth; daughter; cotton weaver; aged 14; born Littleborough
Ellen Firth; daughter; cotton weaver; aged 12; born Walsden
Ada Firth; daughter; scholar; aged 9; born Walsden
Richard Fielden; step son-in-law; cotton weaver; aged 23; unmarried; born Walsden
Mary Fielden; step daughter-in-law; cotton weaver; aged 20; unmarried; born Walsden
Emma Fielden; step daughter-in-law; cotton weaver; aged 17; unmarried; born Walsden
Willie Fielden; step son-in-law; cotton warehouse boy; aged 15; born Walsden

This is a sizeable number of inhabitants for this public house, although the census records who was present when the census was taken and not all may have been resident in the building.

Research into the archives of the *Rochdale Observer* and *Rochdale Times* have not produced any records which date the pub back to an earlier period. John Bamforth, landlord from 1887-1888, died a sudden death at the age of forty-eight, according to the *Rochdale Times* on 9 March 1888 and his wife took over the licence.

The name of the pub changed to the Sportsman's Rest on 18 August 1989. Refer to the Sportsman's Rest for a list of licensees.

DUKE OF YORK

Now a private house in Ealees, this seems to have been the larger of two pubs that supplied the needs of the workers at Ealees Mill and Ealees Colliery. The Duke closed its doors on the 7 January 1943.

On 1 January 1868, an inquest was held at the Rake Inn by J. Molesworth, deputy coroner, on a William Rigg who was found drowned in the lodge opposite the Duke of York. Reports of the inquest record that Sally Hollows was landlady, which pre-dates the record of her tenure previously established.

The *Rochdale Observer* edition of 1 June 1878 reports on a 'horrible case of manslaughter' at the Duke of York of one James Cryer:

On Wednesday evening a most brutal affray, which has had a fatal termination, took place in a beerhouse kept by James Hollows, at Ealees, which is to the right of Halifax Road, Littleborough, shortly after passing under the railway arches. The circumstances are exceptionally shocking. James Cryer, who is about 46 years of age, and was by occupation a knocker-up, residing at Newgate, Caldermoor, a considerable distance on the other side of Littleborough, and had formerly worked at Croft Head Mill, was in the house, and a young man named George Holden, a labourer, about 30 years of age, and residing at Rock Nook, towards Summit, was also there. A quarrel arose between the two men, and Holden commenced to fight after the brutal fashion known as 'tupping', that is running at each other and butting their heads together like sheep. Cryer was a slender man, but Holden is stout and muscular. During the row, Holden butted his head against Cryer's stomach with such force that actually Cryer had his stomach burst, and he was knocked backwards against a form and his neck dislocated. Though so terribly injured he did not lose consciousness, but all his limbs were paralysed. He was taken home in a cab, the landlord of the house accompanying him, and Mr Richards, assistant to Dr MacGill was called in to see him, and gave directions as to what was to be done, and promised to call again in the morning. He was laid in a couch chair till the doctor came, and several times he told his wife that he was done, and that he was killed. When he was taken upstairs after the doctor's visit he said he should never come down again. Deceased appeared to be in great pain about the neck and when examined he cried out. Deceased lingered through the night and was attentively waited upon. He complained a good deal of having no feeling in his limbs, and said his arms and legs did not belong to him. About five o'clock in the morning he seemed better, and talked cheerfully. The following morning the doctor did not come, and, as deceased was very anxious for him to come, his wife left her work and went to Dr MacGill's. While she was away, at about half past eleven, deceased died in the presence of the people who were attending him. The only reference he made to the affray which cost him his life was that he and Holden had been tupping with their heads, and that Holden hit him in the belly, and he went over in a minute. When the body was laid out, under both armpits was found to be quite black; as if by a severe struggle, and his ears were black. The stomach was badly swollen, and also the back of the neck. When the matter was reported to Mr Molesworth, the coroner, he ordered a post-mortem examination, which was made on Thursday night by Dr Pitcairn. The affair has caused a great sensation in the district. Three years ago at Whitsuntide, a woman who resides at Newgate had her husband killed in a similar fight, his back having been broken. The man with whom he was fighting was committed for trial, but was acquitted at the Assizes. Two of Holden's brothers have died violent deaths, having been killed on the railway, one of them in Summit Tunnel. Holden's father and mother are both alive and are decent elderly people. Deceased was esteemed a very quiet, harmless man. He was married but had no children.

The *Rochdale Observer* edition of 25 February 1882 includes the following:

Notice is hereby given that the household furniture and effects being in the beerhouse known as the Duke of York Inn, Ealees, near Littleborough, in the occupancy of Joseph Greenhalgh of the Duke of York Inn aforesaid are the property of Thomas Sutcliffe of Rochdale Brewery and not the property of the said Joseph Greenhalgh dated 13th February 1882. Signed Thomas Sutcliffe and Joseph Greenhalgh.

The Old Duke of York public house, now a private dwelling at Ealees.

Joseph Greenhalgh was grandfather of the society's immediate past president, Jack Trickett. Coincidently the society's current president, Peter Cryer, has resided in The Old Duke since renovating the property after it fell into disuse as a public house. He tells us that he and his wife bought the property in 1969 from one Alan Greenwood who had lived there from 1962 when the last landlady and her sons who lived in the building as tenants, vacated the premises.

The society is informed by the present owner that in one deed, the building is referred to as the Duke of Norfolk.

LIST OF LICENSEES:

1851	Charles Rigg	1901–1904	Joseph Greenhalgh
1868–1878	Sally Hollows	1904–1911	Joseph Crabtree
1878	Sarah Ann Hollows	1911–1924	Abraham Jackson
1878–1879	Joseph Greenhalgh	1924–1929	Kate Jackson
1879–1882	Samuel Lord	1929–1936	Arthur Casson
1882–1890	Joseph Greenhalgh	1936–1943	Elizabeth Cropper
1890–1901	Esther Walsh		

DYERS ARMS

This is on Whitelees Road and its early history and development is given in *Travis' Notes on*

Littleborough as follows:

After the death of James Taylor in 1825, the widow Sarah entered into possession of the property at Whitelees, and shortly afterwards the Dearnley Colliery Company, by their operations underground caused a subsidence of land by mining for coal, the property being injured by giving way. The damage was so apparent that Mrs Taylor making a claim for the same, the Company, without any threat or compulsion paid her £60 as compensation for the injury done, and immediately she proceeded to make the necessary repairs, and at the same time converted two of the dwellings into six cottages. The three-storey bay of the building previously mentioned, in one portion of which a Job Dyer had been working for some time, was now turned into a beerhouse under the name of the 'Dyers Arms', and thence forth Mrs Taylor improved her worldly advantages greatly for the benefit of her children.

We know from the 1861 census that George Taylor was the landlord. Ownership of the building was not necessarily vested in the landlord, as can be seen from an application in the *Rochdale Times* on 1 August 1874 by the then landlord, Robert Fletcher, for a public billiards licence; the owner of the pub was given as John Bulcock. The 1881 census records:

Part White Lees
Robert Fletcher; head; beerhouse keeper & farmer; aged 43; born Littleborough
Sarah Fletcher; wife; aged 43; born Littleborough
James Fletcher; son; clogger's apprentice; aged 15; unmarried; born Littleborough
Frank Fletcher; son; scholar; aged 12; unmarried; born Littleborough
Frances M. Schofield; sister; weaver; aged 29; married; born Littleborough
Arthur Schofield; nephew; scholar; aged 8; born Littleborough
Emma Schofield; niece; scholar; aged 5; born Littleborough
Ann Kershaw; cousin; weaver; aged 22; unmarried; born Littleborough
Alice Kershaw; cousin; cotton cardroom hand; aged 17; unmarried; born Littleborough
Sarah Kershaw; cousin; cotton cardroom hand; aged 15; unmarried; born Littleborough
Eliza Kershaw; cousin; piecer; aged 13; unmarried; born Littleborough

Robert Fletcher was listed in the 1890 trades directory as a beerseller at No. 157 Whitelees Road.

LIST OF LICENSEES:

1825	Sally Taylor	1959-1964	Granville Thomas
1843-1861	George Taylor	1964-1967	Alfred Atherton
1872-1899	Robert Fletcher	1967-1981	William Cox
1899-1915	William Taylor	1981-1985	Peter Okun
1915-1927	James Whatmough Parker	1985-1990	Joseph Lamb
1927-1942	Joe Hartley	1990-1995	Ann Howarth
1942-1944	Charlie Stott	1995-1996	Frank Shelley
1944-1951	Whalley Cardus	1996-1998	Michael Floyd McCarthy
1951-1953	Charles S G Townsend	1998-2000	Richard Grant Whittaker
1953-1954	Joseph Barlow	2000	Joanne Marie Sammon
1954-1955	Fred Stanley Newsome	2000-2005	Janos Lajos Bene-Doszpoly
1955-1959	Kenneth Holmes		

Modern view of the Dyers Arms on Whitelees Road.

Cart advertising Whitbread's ales and wines in 1915.

FALCON INN

On the rear of this building in Littleborough centre, is a date stone of 1657 (inside the present rear porch). This is an indication of the age of one of Littleborough's oldest pubs. Originally built as a farmhouse, it became a major coaching inn of the eighteenth and nineteenth centuries. This is perhaps best illustrated by Tim Bobbin, who in 1757 writes, 'I called at the sign of the Falcon, in Littleborough, where I knew was a glass of good ale, and the landlord a friend to travelling quadrupeds.'

The *Annals of Rochdale* state that the Falcon existed in 1744, but the earliest landlord we have been able to find is Isaac Marsden of the Falcon Inn; this in 1818. However, Alexander Kershaw could have been the landlord in 1676, see the Talbot for this reference. The combined uses as a coaching house and a farm is illustrated in the census of 1851 when it was in the possession of: James Mitchell (thirty-eight); victualler and farmer of eighteen acres.

The *Annals of Todmorden* record a sale by auction at the Queen Hotel, Todmorden on 3 August 1881. Lot three comprised eight freehold dwellings at Swan Place. Together with lots four, five and six, these were sold to John Fletcher of the Falcon Inn for £2,045. The census for 1881 records:

Church Street

John Fletcher; head; publican; aged 44; born Littleborough

Mary Fletcher; wife; aged 50; born Todmorden

Thomas Ashworth; father-in-law; former publican; aged 90; widower; born Todmorden

Frances Williams; general servant; aged 32; unmarried; born Townsend, Cornwall;

Kate Williams; general servant; aged 20; unmarried; born Townsend, Cornwall

The following valuation was taken at the Falcon Inn on the death of John Fletcher in 1889:

20 Gallons of Irish Whiskey	15 Gallons of Scotch Whisky
15 Gallons of Rum	10 Gallons of Gin
2 Gallons of Brandy	8 Gallons of Port Wine
4 Gallons of Sherry Wine	144 Gallons of Beer
18 Gallons of Porter	6 Bottles of Sherry Wine
6 Bottles of Port Wine	10 Boxes of Cigars

Total value of the above; £55 1s 0d

By 1917, Mrs Sarah Ellen Barnes of the Falcon Hotel was able to leave £4,686 on her death.

The Falcon Inn is mentioned again in the *Annals of Todmorden* in 1904, recording the death of the landlord, Mitchell Barnes, late of Todmorden, on 5 September that year, aged sixty-two. He was buried at Cross Stone church, Todmorden, on 8 September.

In the yard at the rear of the Falcon used to be held the Littleborough market. This declined after the Second World War and attempts to reintroduce it were met with strong opposition from market traders in Rochdale.

The old Coach House that was, for many years, England's joiners' workshop is now converted into a heritage centre.

The original stables for the Falcon Inn were converted into three cottages in 1758. The lintel over the door to the middle dwelling records the date of conversion and the initials IMM. We know that the landlord in 1818 was Isaac Marsden (IM). It would probably be too great a

Above left: Rear of the present Falcon Inn, showing the original front façade and entrance.

Above right: Enlargement of part of an aerial photograph of Littleborough. The Falcon, attached cottages and former coaching house to the rear can be clearly seen, together with the covered stalls of the market in the rear yard.

presumption that he was landlord as far back as 1758

References to this public house in the local newspapers include notices of the sale of four shares of £100 in the Broadfield Spinning Co., published in the *Rochdale Observer* on 14 February 1863. The landlord at that time was Abraham Mitchell, which extends the known period of his tenure by two years from that originally recorded. Research now shows that Abraham Mitchell was landlord until his death in 1870. The *Rochdale Observer* on 22 January of that year carried a notice of the auction of livestock belonging to the late Abraham Mitchell by order of his executors. The licence transferred to his wife, Ellen Mitchell who shortly thereafter transferred the licence to one James Mitchell. Later in the same year, the licence was further transferred to Dan Helliwell.

The above indicates that in 1870 the Falcon was still being used as both an inn and a farm. The *Rochdale Observer* reported on 10 February 1883 an auction of farm land belonging to the Falcon Inn, 'due to declining farming business'. This land was to the front of the present public house and constituted what is now the area of Littleborough Square and the Cenotaph. The land was possibly bought by a William Clough and was transferred into the ownership of the Littleborough Local Board in 1887.

In 1886 the then landlord, John Fletcher commissioned local architect F.H. Shuttleworth to design and have erected a dwelling house extension to the inn. This was built at right angles to the rear of the present pub, as an infill between the pub and the coaching house/stables.

LIST OF LICENSEES:

1676–1676	Alex Kershaw	1936–1940	Wilfred Taylor
1818–1824	Isaac Marsden	1940–1941	Charles Whiteley Smith
1843–1845	Joseph Hartley	1941–1946	Mary Ellen Smith
1851–1852	James Mitchell	1946–1956	Charles Whiteley Smith

1858-1870	Abraham Mitchell	1956-1959	Michael Mullaney
1870	Ellen Mitchell	1959-1960	Frank Henderson
1870	James Mitchell	1960-1979	Lawrence McNeil
1870-1873	Dan Helliwell	1980-1982	Thomas Pollock
1873-1879	Mary Helliwell	1982-1987	Liam McCrae
1879-1883	John Fletcher	1987	Sheila Jackson
1883-1884	Champion Greenwood	1987	Michael Smith
1884 1890	John Fletcher	1987	Sheila Jackson
1890	Mrs John Fletcher	1987-1988	Philip Moore
1890-1904	Mitchell Barnes	1988-1989	Raymond Howell
1904-1916	Sarah Ellen Barnes	1989-1990	John Joseph Lydon
1916-1922	Charles Richard Barnes	1990-1992	Sheila Lydon
1922-1929	Wilfred Cryer	1992	Mavis Baker
1929-1931	James Brearley Taylor	1992-2003	Geoffrey Robert Burns
1931-1936	John Greenwood	2003-2005	Julie Burns
1936-1936	Elizabeth Greenwood		

The former coaching house now restored as a visitor centre.

The modern frontage of the Falcon Inn which, when the building was originally constructed, was the rear of the property.

The former Falcon Inn landlord's house; now used for the sale of antiquarian and second-hand books.

FISHERMAN'S INN

This is one of the many pubs that used to surround Hollingworth Lake; only this and the Beach, now 'Millers', remain open. Once again, this provides an example of a combined victualler and farmer as we can see from this extract from the 1851 census, 'Fisherman's Inn. Edward Roberts, 48, victualler and farmer of 12 acres, born in Todmorden.'

The combined income from farming and inn-keeping continued until the end of 1873. On 10 January 1874, the *Rochdale Observer* published details of the auction of the farm by the then landlord, George Wilson, describing it as 'twenty-one acres' and with 'immediate possession'.

Some interesting field names occur in this area, some of which can still be identified:

Spout Field, Riding's Waste, Heald Bank, Little Glead Field, Meadow Under The House, Shrogg, Loom Hole Field, Toad Hole, Would, Ripe Earth, Marl Earth, Stubble Field.

Many of these names can be seen to relate to places in the locality and some to the employment of the nineteenth century.

The *Rochdale Observer* of 6 April 1861, under a headline of 'District Intelligence' reported the facts behind an inquest held at the Fisherman's Inn into the deaths of five persons at Hollingworth Lake:

Hollingworth. Melancholy Boating Accident on Hollingworth Lake. Five Youths Drowned. Last week we briefly mentioned that on Good Friday an accident causing the death of five persons had occurred at Hollingworth Lake. The following are the particulars of the melancholy catastrophe. It seems that a great number of people had come from various parts of the country to spend the day at Hollingworth. There were about forty small boats, besides two steamers on the lake, all of which were floating about in various directions; when suddenly, about four o'clock p.m., two of the small boats came into contact with each other near the centre of the lake. The collision was so violent as to capsize both boats, some 13 persons being precipitated into the lake, which at this place is 16

The former
Fishermans Inn, now
a bistro/wine bar.

or 17 yards deep. Several of the small boats paddled away with praiseworthy alacrity to the scene of the disaster, as did also one of the steamers; but long before any assistance arrived, several of the unfortunate sufferers had sunk to rise no more. Out of the number immersed five were got out alive, but three of them were nearly exhausted. One of the boats contained a party of six persons from Heywood and the other a party from High Crompton. Five of the twelve were drowned ... Lawrence Newall Esq., Henry Newall Esq., Joseph Schofield Esq. of Stubley Hall and Richard Kay Jnr Esq. of Heybrook were dragging till a late hour and others subsequently continued to search for the missing bodies ... the fifth body was not recovered till Saturday afternoon. The deplorable occurrence has excited the most profound sorrow throughout the neighbourhood.

The report of the inquest held at the Fisherman's Inn goes on to recount evidence from the Sladens in respect of the number of boating accidents which occurred on the lake in the previous year as a result of drunkenness. The jury returned a unanimous verdict of accidental death.

Near disaster came in the area of the 'Fish' in 1884, when spray on the lake, during a gale, rose twenty feet high and washed away part of the embankment.

At one time, a toll gate for the Hollingworth Toll Road was situated at the Fisherman's. It was later removed to Bear Hill.

The transfer of licence from Thomas Evans to Fred Storer in 1879 caused the police some concern and they objected to the licence transfer. Fred Storer's tenure at the inn was, however, short-lived and on 12 June 1880 the *Rochdale Times* reported the failure of Fred Storer's business, thus:

Failure of a Hollingworth Publican. Mr E.C. Blakeway, solicitor, Deansgate, Manchester filed a petition for liquidation at the Oldham County Court, on Tuesday, on behalf of Frederick William Storer, of the Fisherman Inn, Hollingworth Lake, licensed victualler. Liabilities £1,100. Mr Edward Hill, The Orchard, Rochdale, has been appointed receiver.

During the winter of 2005-2006 and in the course of compiling this book, the Fisherman's Inn closed down, was refurbished and re-opened as the Wine Press, a pub-bistro.

LIST OF LICENSEES:

1845	James Broadley	1933–1937	George Henry Cross
1848–1852	Richard Roberts	1937–1947	George Henry Stubbing
1858–1869	John Hudson	1947–1965	Kenneth E H Birch
1869	W. Yarwood	1965–1965	Joan W Birch
1872–1875	George Wilson	1965–1973	Geoffrey R Barker
1875–1876	George Yarwood	1973–1981	David Shaw
1876–1878	John Cunliffe	1981–1985	Malcolm Slade
1878–1879	Thomas Cooper Evans	1985–1987	Jack Smith
1879–1880	Frederick William Storer	1987	John Bartey
1880–1894	Henry Wild	1987–1989	Michael Robert Traynor
1894–1895	James Dearden	1989–1990	Stephen Roy Walker
1895–1906	James Milne	1990	Lesley Jane Whitehead
1906–1908	John Earnshaw	1990	Carol Di Carva
1908–1913	James Thomas Leach	1990–1991	John Victor Young
1913–1916	Thomas Mills	1991–1992	Victor Booth
1916–1917	John William Astin	1992–1993	Christopher John Lockwood
1917–1924	John Thomas Leach	1993–2002	Christopher William Holmes
1924–1931	Frank Leach	2002–2005	Brian Lawrence Gannon
1931–1933	Elizabeth Leach		

FRIENDLY ARMS

One of the Littleborough public houses of which very little is known, except for the occasional references in the trade directories and sited, we think, on Hare Hill Road. No doubt it was a beerhouse that eventually became an off-licence and so the name only survived a few years

We do know that the landlord in 1857 was called Butterworth. His wife, Rebecca, in that year was prosecuted for obstructing the police in their investigations of card playing for money.

LIST OF LICENSEES:

1857	Mr Butterworth	1858–1861	George Rigg

GALE INN

Once again we must refer to Travis' *Littleborough Notes* for the most interesting mention of this pub. He describes it in the following manner:

> Soon after the road was made (Todmorden Road), Mr Laurence Newall of Town House, took down an old farmhouse and other buildings and erected 'The Brow', otherwise 'Gale House', and the Gale Inn. When the public house was ready for occupation, it was 'Letten', along with the farm land, to Robert Hill and his wife, who both of them had been servants of the family.
>
> After the death of the old people, the inn was kept by Charles, their son … and after his death, by his sister, Esther, … she later went to keep the Handle Hall public house at which place she died.

Hare Hill Road,
possibly the location
of the Friendly Arms.

There should be a date stone of 1828 but we suspect this is hidden by the modern sign. In confirmation of the Travis' Notes, we find that the 1851 census gives, 'Esther Hill, 36, farmer of 26 acres.'

Another inn with dual occupation; by 1881, this dual occupation had ceased. The census in that year records:

Gale
Hartley Thistlewhite; head; publican; aged 36; born Marsden
Alice Thistlewhite; wife; aged 32; born Marsden
Sarah Thistlewhite; daughter; scholar; aged 10; born Littleborough

As mentioned earlier, inns were popular meeting places and venues for a variety of events. The *Rochdale Star* on 9 November 1888 reported the following details of an inquest held at the Gale Inn by Molesworth, Rochdale Coroner, into the death of a woman injured on the railway crossing at Green Vale:

Death on the Railway at Littleborough. In the small hours of Sunday morning last Robert Stevenson, scutcher, residing at No. 2, Green Vale, Littleborough, discovered a woman named Sarah Ellen Dawson, aged 31, lying upon the railway near Green Vale crossing. She was moaning but seemed to be unconscious, and died shortly after. On Tuesday morning Mr F.N. Molesworth, coroner, held an inquest at the Gale Inn, Littleborough, on the body of deceased. James Dawson, who identified the body as that of his wife, said that he saw her last on Saturday night between six and seven. She said that she was going to a broker's in Littleborough. Deceased was seen soon after eleven o'clock, three hours previously, going along the footpath leading from Todmorden Road to Green Vale. She was shouting and talking to herself. When Stevenson found Dawson, both her legs were nearly cut off below the knee; her body was cut and bruised, and her right hand and left temple were also severely wounded. The jury brought in a verdict to the effect that deceased's death was the result of injuries caused by her being knocked down by a locomotive engine, but there was not sufficient evidence to show how she came there.

Gale, the area each side of Todmorden Road between the centre of Littleborough and Rock Nook.

The former Gale Inn.

Ornate roof tiles which were added after the building closed as a public house.

In 1908, the Annals of Todmorden recorded that the landlord of the Gale Inn, Mr Ellis Greenwood and his son were involved in a serious cycling accident. This did not prevent him from continuing as landlord for a further two years.

At the end of the twentieth-century the Gale Inn was closed and converted into its present day use, the New China Palace, a Chinese restaurant.

LIST OF LICENSEES:

1828	Robert Hill	1911–1917	George Hoyle
1832–1843	Charles Hill	1917–1919	Esther Hoyle
1845–1851	Esther Hill	1919–1929	George Hoyle
1852–1858	Benjamin Kershaw	1929–1931	George Almond
1861	James Cryer	1931–1933	Arthur Schofield
1870–1871	Harry Thistlethwaite	1933–1937	William Taylor
1871	Thomas Law	1937–1940	Kenneth James Magee
1873–1875	Wally Law	1940–1943	George Kershaw
1875	William Fletcher	1943–1945	Cecelia Kershaw
1875–1886	Hartley Thistlewhite	1945–1950	Selina Sutcliffe
1886–1887	Jane Lord	1950–1953	Arthur Greenwood
1887–1888	William Windle	1953–1957	John Robert Carruthers
1888–1893	William Wiltshire	1957–1959	Granville Thomas
1893–1904	John Wadsworth	1959	Ronald Tomlinson
1904–1910	Ellis Greenwood	1959–1972	Edward Lewis
1910	George Hoyle	1972–1974	Mary Lewis
1910–1911	William Hill	1974–1998	Richard James Grounds

GATE INN

This is one of the early names for the Lydgate Inn, where full details can be found. Suffice it to say that the name could derive from the word *yate*, meaning a way or road. As we will see, it is a gate that hangs well. Refer to the Lydgate Inn for a list of licensees.

GOLDEN FLEECE

This appears only once in the directories, in that for 1879. It does not appear in the licensing records. The directory gives Robert Hurst & Co., Golden Fleece, Church Street

This is almost certainly the Hurst of the Wheat Sheaf, who may have opened this inn as a stop-gap during the rebuilding of the Sheaf. We believe it to have been in Littleborough although there are Golden Fleeces mentioned in Milnrow and Smallbridge. The finding of the Golden Fleece is purported to bring wealth. Good Luck!

LIST OF LICENSEES:

1879	Robert Hurst

Church Street, Littleborough. It is thought that the Golden Fleece was somewhere in this location.

HANDLE HALL

Originally the residence of the lords of the manor, this building later became a slaughterhouse, until the late 1980s. It is now converted into private dwellings.

The Dearden family originated in the farm across the road, known as Whitfield and came into possession of the manor after serving time as stewards to Lord Byron.

The history of the pub will be found under the Queen Anne Inn, where will also be found a list of licensees.

HARE AND HOUNDS, CLEGG HALL

As previously mentioned, this was one of the names for the pub at Clegg Hall, the relevant notes, together with a list of licensees will be found under that name.

HARE AND HOUNDS, DEARNLEY

No licensing records for this public house exist. It is mentioned only once in other records that we have and that is in 1856. On 4 October that year, the *Rochdale Observer* carried a notice, 'To let, beerhouse, Hare & Hounds, New Road, Dearnley, apply Charles Turner on premises.'

With further research it could be discovered that this was the forerunner of the Blue Bell, also a beerhouse on New Road, Dearnley. As noted earlier, the first record of a landlord for this latter establishment in 1858, two years after the auction referred to above.

LIST OF LICENSEES:

1858   Charles Turner

Handle Hall, Calderbrook – former hall, public house and abattoir; now private dwellings.

The A58 at Dearnley; possible location of the Hare and Hounds public house

HAYRAKE

The original form of the name of the Rake Inn gives us a good clue to the origin of this pub. Although it may at one time have been a coaching inn, its regulars would undoubtedly have come from the farms above the inn.

The name derives from the simple farm utensil and not from the man of fashion, or debauched and dissolute person that some signwriters would have us believe.

Refer to the Rake Inn for full details and a list of licensees.

HORSESHOE, FEATHERSTALL

Situated at the bottom of Whitelees Road, where the entrance to Whittle Street now is, this inn appears to have been, at one time, a weaver's cottage with an upper floor of mullioned windows. This is probably the pub that Waugh describes as, 'An old-fashioned public house, apparently as old as Stubley Hall.'

The earliest record gives William Townley, victualler in 1821; the licence expired on the 12 December 1909. The 1861 census records, 'Robert Rigg; inn keeper; Featherstall; aged 56.' The 1881 census records:

Featherstall
George Rigg; head; inn keeper; aged 52; widower; born Littleborough
George Rigg; son; fulling miller; aged 27; unmarried; born Littleborough
Mary Rigg; daughter; domestic servant; aged 25; unmarried; born Littleborough
Elizabeth Rigg; daughter; servant; aged 17; born Littleborough
Edward Rigg; son; cotton mill hand; aged 13; unmarried; born Littleborough
Jesse Rigg; son; scholar; aged 9; born Littleborough

It may be interesting to note that the house next door, or next but one, was the original starting place for the Featherstall Workingman's Club, a coincidence when we look at the next pub.

On 8 February 1896, the *Rochdale Times* carried a report of a meeting of the creditors of the 'former' landlord.

From maps of this area, we have deduced that this public house stood on land which later became part of Henry Whittles' bakery empire.

LIST OF LICENSEES:

1821	William Townley	1858–1879	Robert Rigg
1823–1824	Thomas Butterworth	1879	John Hoyle
1837	Jeremiah Fletcher	1879–1882	George Rigg
1843	Alice Fletcher	1882–1896	Thomas Bentley
1845	Henry Fitton	1896–1900	William Holt
1848	Abraham Grindrod	1900–1901	Ellen Holt
1851–1852	John Rigg	1901–1909	Joseph Butterworth

The Horseshoe
at Featherstall,
purveyors of
Empress Ales.

Whittles Street,
over the entrance to
which once stood
the Horseshoe
public house.

HORSESHOE, LITTLEBOROUGH

The second Horseshoe is now the Trades Hall Club, opposite the parish church, with the name
still carved in the stonework over the door. The name is also perpetuated by having a horseshoe
emblazoned on the club pullover.

The 1881 census records:

Horse Shoe, Church Street
Robert Horrocks; head; blacksmith and beerseller; aged 50; born Littleborough
Elizabeth Horrocks; wife; aged 50; born Whitworth
James Horrocks; son; blacksmith; aged 21; unmarried; born Whitworth
John Robert Horrocks; son; butcher's apprentice; aged 17; unmarried; born Whitworth
Samuel Horrocks; son; clogger (apprentice); aged 14; unmarried; born Whitworth

Now Littleborough Trades Hall Working Men's Club, the former Horseshoe public house.

In 1917 the horseshoe was converted to the present club detailed in the *Rochdale Observer* for 19 January 1918, 'The conversion of the Horseshoe Hotel, Church Street, Littleborough into a Trades Hall by the Littleborough Trades and Labour Council, in November, was of considerable value to the labour movement.'

Also in the *Rochdale Observer*, 1889, 'County police stationed in Littleborough raided the Horseshoe Inn on the day of the Manchester Cup. Samuel Lord and twenty-one visitors were arrested for gambling, betting on horses. Lord was fined £25 with the cost of three court appearances. Had the bets been paid, Lord would have won £16.' What would the same magistrate would have said today when it is possible to win £100 for 10p in the same building and then go next door and legally bet on the horses?

In 1910 a mining disaster at Over Hulton Pit saw widespread fund raising to assist those widowed and orphaned by the disaster. The *Rochdale Observer* on 4 January 1911 reported, '*Rochdale Observer* Shilling Fund for Widows and Orphans of Over Hulton Pit disaster, whip-round at Horse Shoe Inn, Church Street, realises 13/-.'

LIST OF LICENSEES:

1872-1874	Thomas Wild	1890-1891	James Barker
1874	Esau Barker	1891-1913	John Beresford
1874-1887	Robert Horrocks	1913-1914	Sarah Elizabeth Beresford
1887-1889	Samuel Lord	1914-1915	William Bentley
1889-1890	John Hoyle	1915	Ann Bentley

HUNTSMAN

Originally the Royal Oak, Summit, the name was changed to the Huntsman in 1962. This public house is another of those built to supply the needs of this industrial and densely populated area of Summit, or as it was known in earlier times – Wilderness. The 1881 census records:

Royal Oak Inn, Wilderness

Mary Thomas; head; landlady & farmer; aged 41; widow; born Littleborough

Sarah E. Thomas; daughter; assistant to innkeeper; aged 18; unmarried; born Littleborough

Lucy H. Thomas; daughter; assistant to innkeeper; aged 15; unmarried; born Littleborough

Emmaline Thomas; daughter; cotton weaver; aged 14; unmarried; born Littleborough

Robert Thomas; son; scholar; aged 10; born Littleborough

Willie Thomas; son; scholar; aged 8; born Littleborough

Not much is recorded about the history of the pub. The *Rochdale Observer* of 15 July 1871 reported:

> Sudden Death. John Molesworth Esq., held an inquest on Saturday, at the Royal Oak Summit, on the body of William Shore, aged 64 years, cotton operative, who died suddenly on the 7th inst., at his residence, Rock Nook. Deceased went out with a cart on the day named and was suddenly taken ill on his way home and died some few minutes after arriving there. After the deceased's death Dr Lister was called in. The jury returned a verdict of death from natural causes.

Unfortunately, the report does not give details of the landlord and we are therefore unable to determine whether John Thomas' tenure extended back before 1872. In 1897 it was reported that one Thomas Edward Riley of the Royal Oak, Summit was found drowned. He was not the landlord. It is recorded in the licensing records that the landlord of the Huntsman was fined £400 plus £45 costs in 1996 for allowing drinking after hours.

LIST OF LICENSEES:

1872–1877	John Thomas	1971–1984	Theresa Crabtree
1877–1900	Mary Thomas	1984–1988	Peter Hopkinson
1900–1922	Harry Bamford	1988–1990	James Whipp
1922–1947	Thomas Duckworth	1990	Pauline Serena Grounds
1947–1956	Mary Ann Duckworth	1990–1995	Edward Wroe
1956–1971	Roy Crabtree	1995–2005	Ian Scott Hastie

KING WILLIAM IV

Known locally as the King Bill, this inn lies on one of the old roads that were used by traders crossing the moors in this part of Lancashire. In fact, that part of the road down from the King Bill to Starring is known as 'Th' Owd Shef'. Note that this refers to a part of a road and not an old pub.

A variety of occupations was available to the early occupants of the King Bill as can be seen from extracts from the 1851 census:

James Bamford head, 51, Innkeeper

Ann Bamford wife, 46 from Wakefield

James Midwood son, 33, Joiner

Ann Midwood dau. in law, 23, born in Nottingham

William Hollas, 14, Nephew, Warehouse boy

The Huntsman on Todmorden Road at Summit.

The King William IV or 'King Bill' public house.

In an article headlined 'The danger of butcher's garbage', the *Rochdale Observer* of 7 September 1872 detailed an inquest held at the pub the previous Monday:

> John Molesworth, Esq. held an inquest on Monday evening at the King William Inn, Lower Shore, on the body of the infant son of John Smith, cotton operative, residing at Calf Edge, near Shore. From the evidence of the father it appeared that deceased was born on the previous Wednesday evening and it was apparently a healthy child. On Saturday, however, it became unwell and appeared to be in a fit. Dr Lister was sent for but deceased had expired 40 minutes before he arrived. In the course of the corroborative evidence, it appeared that a quantity of butcher's garbage had been removed close to the residence of deceased parents and from this refuse an offensive smell arose. Several of the jury complained of the stench and in returning their verdict of death from natural causes they recommended that the local board should interfere to prevent the removal of garbage without it being previously disinfected.

In 1878, with Hannah Marshall as landlady, the *Rochdale Observer* reported a party held at the King William IV for forty workers of James Fletcher & Bros, flannel manufacturers of Higher Shore. The census for 1881 gives:

Lower Shore
Hannah Marshall; head; inn keeper; aged 48; widow; born Erringden, York
John Marshall; son; fulling miller; aged 21; unmarried; born Stansfield, York
Mary Ann Marshall; daughter; domestic servant; aged 19; unmarried; born Stansfield, York
Collinge Marshall; son; clogger; aged 14; unmarried; born Stansfield, York

The *Rochdale Times* on 5 June 1897 reported the suicide of William Clayton, landlord of the King William IV, thus:

> Shocking Suicide at Shore; The Landlord of the 'King William' Cuts His Throat. Sergeant Gilbody reports the death of William Clayton, publican, of King William the Fourth Inn, Shore. Deceased, it appears, had been drinking heavily of late, and his wife had requested him several times not to drink to excess. He had been very low-spirited lately. About twelve o'clock noon on the 2nd inst. Dr MacGill attended deceased, and told his wife not to let him have any more drink. At 4.45 p.m. deceased, along with his family, had tea together, after which deceased went out, saying he would go into the brewhouse. Finding deceased did not return in a reasonable time, Mrs Clayton went out and found him lying on his stomach in the brewhouse. She at once called for assistance, and deceased's brother, Samuel Clayton, went and found deceased with his throat cut and a large carving-knife by his side. The knife was very sharp, and had the appearance of having been newly ground. Dr Ballantyne was sent for, but when he arrived deceased had expired.

Records do not show who became licensee until 1878 with the tenure of David Whitley.
    A record in the society archives gives details of the range and prices of drinks on sale in the 'King Bill' in around 1962:

Mild beer ... pint	1s 3d	Cointreau	3s 6d
Shandy ... pint	1s 8d	Cherry Brandy	2s 6d
Pale Ale	1s 1d	Advocaat	2s 3d

Make the best of your leisure at the

King William the Fourth Inn
SHORE, LITTLEBOROUGH.

Only the Finest Ales, Stout, Wines
and Spirits, supplied by the

CROWN BREWERY CO. LTD., BURY.

Advertisement for the King Bill from a 1935 edition of *Littleborough Shopping Weekly.*

XX	11d	Egg Flip	1s 6d
Crystal	10½d	Sloe Gin	2s 3d
Worthington	1s 5½d	Tia Maria	2s 6d
Bass	1s 5½d	Drambuie	3s 6d
Guinness	1s 4d	Benedictine	3s 6d
Mackeson	1s 4½d	Orange & Soda	6d
Nut Brown	1s 3d	Black beer & lemon	1s
Babycham	1s 3d	Minerals	6d & 1s
Rum	2s 1d	Lime	2d
Whisky	2s 1d	Peppermint	2d
Brandy	2s 6d	Orange	2d

LIST OF LICENSEES:

1848–1848	James Bamford	1931–1934	Jessie Surrage
1852–1852	Ann Bamford	1934–1951	Silvester Haughton
1861–1861	Edmund Leach	1951–1952	Doris May Haughton
1872–1873	John Howarth	1952–1954	Frank Hayhurst
1873–1877	William Marshall	1954–1956	David Arthur Drinkwater
1877–1884	Hannah Marshall	1956–1967	John William Forth
1884–1897	William Clayton	1967–1971	Nellie Forth
1898–1904	David Whitley	1971–1973	Frank Kirk
1904–1908	Emma Whitley	1973–1983	Thomas Albert Edwards
1908–1921	Robert Brierley	1983	Edna Edwards
1921–1924	John Sutcliffe	1983–1999	Frank Findlow
1924–1925	John Russell	1999	Lynne Cramb
1925–1926	William Henry Whittall	1999–2000	Sandra Hurst
1927–1928	John Chadwick	2000–2002	April Trainor
1928–1931	Samuel Haughton	2002–2005	Sandra Kerr

LAKE HOTEL

At the back of Hollingworth Lake, this hotel, with its dancing stages and Swiss style buildings, was developed in the hey-day of Victorian popularity for the lake and its surroundings. A Mr C.W. Thompson was the earliest recorded owner in 1861 of what, by the 1890s, became part of the Sladen 'empire' of leisure facilities at Hollingworth Lake. It is recorded that the gardens to the hotel were laid out in May 1861 and in June 1863 the building was illuminated by gas.

An advertisement of 1889 gives, 'Lake Hotel; Hollingworth Lake; Under New Management; Uriah Sladen; Late of Beach Hotel.' A previous advertisement in the 1870s, placed collectively by proprietors of the several Hollingworth Lake establishments promises such spectacular events as blindfold swimming and walking the greasy pole (to win a live pig!).

By the 1920s, the owners of the Lake Hotel, Oldham and Rochdale Joint Managing Co., were letting the premises to Rathbone Bros of Stretford, barge builders.

In 1939, the renewal of a licence was refused because of structural deficiencies; it still, however, managed to serve as a restaurant for some thirty years, but was eventually demolished in about 1970. This hotel is, of course, the one that stood in the woods behind the lake, the foundations can still be found.

The popularity of this pub was based on its location and served the growing numbers of tourists who came to visit Hollingworth Lake. Its decline matched a decline in the number of visitors to the lake and in its final years was unfit to be licensed but was able to continue serving non-alcoholic refreshments to those who walked or took the ferry to the back of the lake.

LIST OF LICENSEES:

1861	C.W. Thompson	1922-1924	James Sladen
1863-1873	George Yarwood	1924-1925	George William Ruberry
1873-1882	William Worth	1925-1926	Gerald Parker
1882-1885	Edward Woolfenden	1926-1930	Elliot Lees Buckley
1885-1888	John Cockroft	1930-1931	Arthur Morton
1888-1889	Mary Mills	1931-1932	Richard Hartley
1889-1918	Uriah Sladen	1932-1939	Ethel Buckley
1918-1922	Eliza Sladen		

LANCASHIRE & YORKSHIRE HOTEL

The origin of this hotel at Hollingworth Lake can be traced to the purchase of 600 square yards of land from a gentleman by the name of Harding, by a certain William Whipp, in 1872. By the year 1874, Thomas Whipp was the owner of 'a dancing stage and ticket office' and, in 1881, the Whipp family sold to Joseph Clegg 'all that Hotel or Public House, Dancing Stage, stables and other buildings' for £2,200. A sales notice of 1888 describes the premises as follows:

> The Hotel, which is well adapted for doing a large business, has a large and commanding frontage, is three storeys high and contains 23 rooms. The lake, being a popular holiday resort, the takings at Easter, which is close at hand, and other holiday seasons are very great.

H OLLINGWORTH LAKE.

GREAT NATIONAL SWIMMING RACES AND
EXHIBITION OF LIFE SAVING APPARATUS
IN CASE OF SHIPWRECK.
ON SATURDAY, JULY 7TH, 1877,
NEGRO PEARL DIVERS.
BOAT, TUB, AND CANOE RACES,
by Negroes and White Men.
BLINDFOLD SWIMMING RACES,
by Professor Bibbero and his Pupils.
WALKING GREASY POLE FOR LIVE PIG.
A MONSTER DUCK HUNT
and numerous other Attractions, for Particulars of which and
Prizes, see Bills.
Visitors will find ample accomodation for both Man and
Horse at the following Hotels, viz.
MR. WM. WORTH, Lake Hotel.
MR. U. SLADEN, Beech Hotel.
MR. WM. WRIPP, Lancashire and Yorkshire Hotel.
MR. JNO. CUNLIFF, Fisherman's Inn.
MR. GEO. SWINDELL'S Refreshment Rooms,
Yorkshire House. 1033
Cheap Trains at Reduced Fares. See Companies Bills. g

Above: The Lake Hotel, photographed on 29 January 1939.

Left: Advertisement from the 1870s for several attractions at Hollingworth Lake.

Below: Information Centre at the back of the lake, close to the site of the Lake Hotel.

JAMES SLADEN,
BEACH HOTEL, HOLLINGWORTH LAKE,
SELLS
RUM, GIN,
WHISKEY, AND BRANDY,
In Large and Small Bottles.

LANCASHIRE & YORKSHIRE HOTEL
(NEAR THE LANDING STAGE),
HOLLINGWORTH LAKE.
VISITORS to this far-famed and picturesque resort will find
the above Establishment replete with every accommodation for
their pleasure and comfort.
The Proprietor has, regardless of expense, made extensive
alterations in and about the house, and fitted up one of the
most extensive and convenient DANCING PLATFORMS in
the country, covering an area of 18,360 superficial square feet.
BAND in ATTENDANCE DAILY, and TWO THIS DAY.—
MRS. WESTON, Pianist and Vocalist,
DINNERS, TEAS, SANDWICHES,
and other Refreshments.
ALES, PORTER, WINES, AND CIGARS.
WILLIAM WHIPP, Proprietor.

Above left: The Lancashire & Yorkshire Hotel at the heyday of Hollingworth Lake as a tourist resort.

Above right: Advertisements placed in the *Rochdale Observer* for the Beach Hotel and Lancashire & Yorkshire Hotel.

Left: Site of the Lancashire & Yorkshire Hotel on Lake Bank.

At this time there was based in the area, a company called the Hollingworth Lake & Gardens Co., formed to promote the leisure activities at the lake (liquidated in 1886) which was accused, in its early days, of, 'Disfiguring the picturesqueness of the lake by creating a large hoarding near the L & Y Hotel.'S

The licence for the hotel expired on 21 December 1911. We have been unable to ascertain when the building was demolished, though it is recorded that the building was bought on 8 August 1910 for £755 by a H. Rawson of the Brittania Hotel on Lomax Street, Rochdale. We do know that the stone which was salvaged from the demolition of the hotel was used in the construction of the houses that now stand on the site.

The dancing platform referred to had dimensions of 18,360 sq.ft. According to an advertisement placed in the *Rochdale Observer* on 14 June of that year. The pub did not get a full spirits licence until 1878.

On 3rd December 1881, the *Rochdale Times* reported that a large dinner was held at the Lancashire & Yorkshire Hotel for 102 hands employed by Hall & Rodgers to celebrate the twenty-first birthday of James Taylor Rodgers. Hall & Rodgers, who continue trading to this day as builders' merchants, owned a brick and tile manufacturing business on land alongside the Rochdale Canal in Smithy Bridge. The site is now occupied by the houses of Walmsley Avenue.

LIST OF LICENSEES:

1872–1883	William Whipp	1886–1890	John Hudson
1883–1885	Nancy Hambler	1890–1910	Levi Lord
1885	John Littlewood	1910–1911	Robert Butterworth
1885	John Henry Martin		

LODGE INN

Behind Hollingworth Lake, on the road to Rakewood, stands Lodgeville house, which used to be the Lodge Inn. When it commenced trading as an inn is not clear, but there is a date stone of 1826, and in Littleborough churchyard is a memorial to, 'Henry Wood, late of the Lodge Inn, Hollingworth Lake, Innkeeper, who died on the 6th day of April 1845, aged 26 years.'

By 1851, the inn was occupied by Simeon Lord, his wife, three children and four lodgers. This same Simeon Lord was a farmer of thirty acres.

An interesting note, relating to the period 1842-1847, refers to the Toll Road around this side of the lake. It appears that travellers who went via the Lodge Inn, had to pay at the Toll Bar, but those who went to the Mermaid, had no need to pay the toll.

The reason that travellers to the Mermaid (see later) did not pay a toll was that the toll gate for this road was set at the bottom of Bear Hill. Access to the Mermaid Inn and Hollingworth Fold generally was made just before passing through the toll gate which controlled the private road through to Rakewood.

In 1868 the landlord, Richard Slinger, was prosecuted for allowing gaming in his public house. Prior to that, a record in the society archives shows that in 1858 the landlord and three others were fined for organising a 'main' or cock-fight.

On 27 October 1894 and again on 18 April 1896, the *Rochdale Times* reported auctions held at the Lodge Inn, of livestock 'due to declining farming business', with James Milne and Charles Holt as respective landlords.

In the *Rochdale Observer* of 1921, a local ratepayer was complaining about the lack of lights near the Lodge Inn, the street lamps having been removed during the First World War. The inn closed in 1916 although the licence did not expire until 14 February 1917, when there was no application for renewal.

LIST OF LICENSEES:

1845	Henry Wood	1895–1896	Charles Holt
1851	Simeon Lord	1896–1904	Benjamin Chadwick
1852	Ralph Eastham	1904–1905	John Thomas Massey
1858–1872	Richard Slinger	1905–1907	Thomas Allen
1872–1889	Solomon Butterworth	1907–1911	Thomas Henry Warburton
1889–1891	Alfred Wild	1911–1914	Arthur Herbert Kitchen
1891–1895	James Milne	1914–1915	William Heseltine
1895	Betty Milne	1915–1917	Arthur Heseltine

Rakewood, which still retains part of the old mill industry that was very much a part of Littleborough's Victorian past.

Private dwellings, formerly The Lodge Inn serving the local Rakewood inhabitants.

LYDGATE INN

Although the earliest reference to the inn that we have been able to find is for 1818, when James Wrigley, victualler and reed maker, lived at Lydgate Gate, there is no doubt in our minds that this would have been a stopping place for travellers over Blackstone Edge, before that time.

Some early variations of the name include Lydiet Inn, Lytgate Inn, Gate Tavern and Gate Inn. The famous sign that used to hang at the inn showed a pleasant valley and the words, 'This gate hangs well, and hinders none; refresh and pay and travel on.'

This quotation appears at a number of pubs in England, particularly at the Gate Inn at Yanwath in the Lake District.

The 1881 census records:

Lydgate:
Alice Palfryman; head; licensed victualler; aged 56; widow; born Carlton, York
Jno Palfryman; son; farm servant; aged 34; married; born Carlton, York
Jane Palfryman; daughter-in-law; aged 34; married; born Kildwick, York
John Stott; lodger; general labourer; aged 62; unmarried; born Littleborough

The Lydgate Inn on Blackstone Edge Old Road. The pub sign with the gate and inscription clearly visible.

Law's Lydgate Mill, now converted into apartments.

High Peak, housing built by the Law Family for workers at Lydgate Mill and taking its name from the parliamentary constituency represented for several years by Alfred Law.

The Lydgate as it stands today, converted into a private dwelling.

By 1895, the inn was part of the Law's estate and as far as we can ascertain, it was never taken over by a brewery.

The early development of a mill industry in Littleborough started in the surrounding hills at places such as Lydgate, Shore and Clough. Only with advances in technology was it possible for mill owners to relocate to the valley floor and more accessible transportation. Lydgate Mill was such an example. The Law family started their fulling operations at a mill built next door to the Lydgate Inn, relocating to Durn Mill on the valley floor beneath the Lydgate when the canal opened up transport routes to Hull and Liverpool.

An interesting souvenir of a reunion of the Gatehouse Rangers Football Club of 1909, held at the Gate Inn, Lydgate, gives the following menu for the dinner, 'Roast Beef, Boiled Potatoes; Roast Mutton, Peas; Currant Pudding; Cheese, Biscuits, Celery'. The occasion was a visit, on a return from Canada, of Tom Fletcher, an 'old boy' of the team.

The Lydgate closed as a public house in the 1980s and after a period, was converted into a dwelling house. It was used in the 1980s as the setting for an episode of *The Travelling Man*, a television series starring Leigh Lawson.

LIST OF LICENSEES:

1818	James Wrigley	1899–1907	Jane Palfreyman
1832	James Hill	1907–1912	William Hill
1843	Stephen Howard	1912–1917	John Hartley Hill
1848–1851	Abraham Rogers	1917–1932	William Fletcher
1851–1852	Jonas Pearson	1932	Hannah Fletcher
1861	James Parker	1932–1942	Isaac Rushton
1870	Sarah Baker	1975–1977	David Graham Kershaw
1870–1875	Thomas Palfryman	1977–1978	William Mount
1875–1899	Alice Palfryman	1978–1983	David Graham Kershaw

MERMAID INN

On the old road out of Hollingworth Lake to Ogden, this inn must have been the last place of refreshment until the Rams Head on the Denshaw Road for travellers and traders who had reason to go through Hollingworth and Schofield.

The directory of 1818 is the earliest record we have of the inn, but it must have existed before this to serve the then populous hamlet of Hollingworth. Little is recorded of this public house. In 1857, we find a William Hill in occupation, offering to let the inn, details to be provided on application. In 1873, George Travis (late collier) was advertising in *Worral's Directory* and was offering, 'The Inn, delightfully situated on the summit of a hill at the top of the lake, commanding a beautiful view on the same and surrounding scenery. And good stabling.'

As late as 1907, the executors of the Abraham Dearden who died in the December of 1903, were publishing notices regarding his estate in the *Rochdale Times*. Abraham Dearden was described as former stone merchant and publican.

The inn was closed in 1911 and was apparently demolished in the 1940s.

LIST OF LICENSEES:

1818–1823	John Shore	1892–1898	James Fielden
1851	John Whittle	1898–1900	Edmund Farrow
1852	John Rhodes	1900–1902	Thomas Wild
1857	William Hill	1902–1903	Abraham Dearden
1858	James Sladen	1903–1906	Hannah Dearden
1861	M. Lord	1906–1907	Benjamin Feather
1869	Henry Taylor	1907–1908	George Crabtree
1869–1892	George Travis	1908–1911	Robert Lee

MILLERS

This is the current name of the former Beach Hotel, which was re-branded and externally redecorated in the early part of this century. Refer to the Beach Hotel for a fuller history and details of the licensees.

Above: The Mermaid Inn, one of a cluster of buildings at Hollingworth Fold, now demolished.

Right: Hollingworth Fold, with foliage replacing several of the old buildings.

MINERS ARMS

This was a house at Ealees, possibly No.1 Ealees. We have seen no record of this in either the directories or licensing records. It is possible that it was used to serve the miners at Ealees Colliery, before the time that the Duke of York came to be built.

An owner of the house at No. 1 Ealees, in the 1990s confirmed that his deeds showed that the property had once been known as the Miners Arms. No records of any licensees have survived.

THE MOORCOCK

This inn was originally Swaindrod Farm and seems to have been first licensed in about 1840, as we have the first landlord to be a Thomas Butterworth in 1843. The 1861 census lists, 'John Greenwood; inn keeper and farmer; Lower Swainrod; aged 54.'

The inn, situated at the side of the main Rochdale to Halifax road was firstly a coaching inn. The *Rochdale Times* of 6 August 1881 carried an article reporting the final journey of Hudson's stage coach, recording that the horses were changed at The Moorcock. The census of 1881 records:

Moorcock Inn, Swain Road
John Cryer; head; innkeeper and farmer of 17 acres; aged 37; born Littleborough
Ann Cryer; wife; aged 38; born Littleborough
Fanny T. Cryer; daughter; scholar; aged 10; born Littleborough
William Collinge; servant; fulling miller; aged 22; married; born Littleborough
Emma Collinge; domestic servant; aged 26; married; born Tuxford, Nottingham
Thomas Chadwick; lodger; stone mason; aged 36; unmarried; born Littleborough
Thomas William Schofield; lodger; masons labourer; aged 18; unmarried; born Littleborough

A report in the *Rochdale Observer* of 2 May 1868 records an application for licence by James Collinge, having previously been refused due to the applicants poor past record, state of attire and cleanliness. The *Rochdale Observer* reported the death of the landlord, Thomas Tuson on 3 July 1897, noting that he had been coachman to Captain Beswicke-Royds of Pike House.

In the early 1920s, a poem was written entitled *A Descriptive Account of the Company at the Moorcock Inn, Blackstone Edge*:

Along the road to Blackstone Edge, there stands a little pub;
And the company there can do anything, from playing dominoes to drawing sub.
Amongst this noted company, there are characters of renown:
But one there is who has pride of place, and is the first name to go down.

Of course you know to whom I refer, 'tis our good old friend George Platt;
He goes about contented, with all troubles under one hat.
He's the star turn of the company, but sometimes turns up late;
But of course we have to excuse him because he painted the gate.

And it needs some careful watching; people come from far and near
To see this famous Jazz-gate, it makes them take to beer.

Upon the walls of the 'Moorcock', there stands his photo there —
A picture of contentment, with a smile, that hasn't a care.

Next to him I must place his rival, that is, 'good old Preston Dick',
When in form he is pleasant company, he's such a cant old brick.
He comes from poor, proud Preston, but he's proud to be her son;
And I'm sure we'll all be sorry, when the waterworks are done.

For we shall miss him sorely, his wit, his jokes, his songs;
But he will never leave behind him a multitude of wrongs.
The next that I must mention is 'Jim' of Worcester fame;
He prides himself as Preston's pal, and always stands for the same.

This piece it would not be complete unless I mention one —
He's a gentleman we all respect, and who likes a bit of fun.
I refer to our old friend John Greenwood, whom we are always glad to see,
He pays us frequent visits, and we're all fond of his company.

And now I'm at a loss for words to describe our next star turn;
He's a foreigner from Wardle, but he came to live at Durn.
He's as full of mischief as they make 'em, but he loves his pal, George Platt;
But George loves him best when the cuckoo sings, and no one will deny that.

He's very absent-minded, but doesn't create a fuss;
The other day he lost his mackintosh with riding about in the bus.
And then there are 'Smiths' of Macclesfield, who treat us very well;
I'm sure everybody's satisfied with the goods they send to sell.

And now there is the Landlord, who's as quaint as anyone;
He never seems contented unless something's going on.
But he's quite a decent fellow, and we pull together well:
And I'm sure there isn't nicer company this side of the gates of H---.

The poet signed himself T.A.L. The landlord at that time was William Wild (1917-1923). The Smiths of Macclesfield referred to in the poem was the brewery. We are not sure who the 'company' were.

In its latter days, The Moorcock became a nightclub, with late licence and used to offer free transport from the centre of Littleborough at closing time for the normal public houses. It was later converted into a restaurant.

LIST OF LICENSEES:

1843-1843	Thomas Butterworth	1913	Nanny Haigh
1851	Sarah Hill	1913-1914	William Crabtree
1861-1867	John Greenwood	1914-1917	James Fielden
1867-1869	James Collinge	1917-1923	William Wild
1869	Ann Collinge	1923-1935	Thomas Charles Smith
1872	Robert Butterworth	1936-1941	John Willie Warren

The house at Ealees which was once the Miners Arms.

Ealees, a small hamlet on the edge of central Littleborough.

Above: The Moorcock Inn, now a bar and restaurant.

Right: Poem written about the regular drinkers at the Moorcock Inn.

A Descriptive Account of
the Company at the

MOORCOCK INN,

BLACKSTONEDGE.

Along the road to Blackstonedge
There stands a little pub ;
And the company there can do any-
thing,
From playing dominoes to drawing
sub.

Amongst this noted company
There are characters of renown :
But one there is who has pride of
place,
And is the first name to go down.

Of course you know to whom I refer,
'Tis our good old friend George
Platt ;
He goes about contented,
With all troubles under one hat.

He's the star turn of the company,
But sometimes turns up late ;
But of course we have to excuse him
Because he painted the gate.

1872-1876	Ashworth Greenwood	1941-1950	Edith Bullock
1876-1879	John Greenwood	1951-1953	Harry Evans
1879-1882	John Cryer	1953-1969	Harold Tonge
1882-1883	Abraham Spencer	1969-1975	May Tonge
1883-1891	William Rigg	1975-1980	Joan Bottomley
1891-1896	Joseph Kirby Miles	1980-1981	George Howarth
1896-1897	Thomas Tuson	1981-1984	Michael Lawrence Gorse
1897-1899	Margaret Tuson	1984	Michael Hodgson
1899-1907	Herbert Gibson	1984-1999	Wanda Elizabeth Burke
1907-1910	John Willie Dawson	1999-2005	Pauline Ashworth
1910-1913	William Rigg		

MUSICIANS ARMS

Basically a moor-enders pub, this was on the outskirts of Littleborough and no doubt served the small hamlets of Smithy Nook and Salley Street, along with the farms on this end of Shore Moor.

The 1861 census records a Mary Lord as beerseller (widow) aged 69, of Smithy Nook. Further investigation of the licensing records has revealed a transfer of licence in 1870 from Sarah Ann Cryer to Henry Rogers.

Prior to 1920 this inn was owned by Hargreaves, Coal Merchants. According to the licensing records, the last licensee was a Charles Sumner, although there seems to be some doubt about this.

Calderbrook; Lighthouse looking towards Smithy Nook.

Salley Street at the edge of Shore Moor.

Private house, once known as the Musicians Arms.

Although not recorded as either landlady or wife of the landlord, a Mrs H.T. Milne, late of the Musicians Arms, Calderbrook was interred at Huddersfield Cemetery on 16 December 1931.

The building stands today, converted to a private dwelling.

LIST OF LICENSEES:

1861	Mary Lord	1908-1915	Josiah Thomas
1870	Sarah Ann Cryer	1916	George Chadwick
1870-1885	Henry Rogers	1916-1920	Greenwood Hargreaves
1885-1889	Thomas Welcome Cryer	1920-1926	Herbert Law
1889-1900	Harry Fletcher	1926-1930	William Firth
1900-1906	James Travis	1930-1931	Joseph Thomas
1907	Jane Travis	1931-1933	Emma Doust
1907-1908	John Hartley	1933-1935	Charles William Summers

MUSICIANS INN

The original name for this pub was the Three Horse Shoes, the name being changed to the Musicians Inn in 1875 and by the time of the census of 1881 was known as the Musicians Arms. The inn closed in 1907 when the licence expired on the 9 October that year. It is now a private house.

The 1881 census records:

Musicians Arms, Halifax Road
Enoch Gibson; head; beerseller; aged 67; born Stansfield, York
Betty Gibson; wife; beerseller; aged 67; born Walsden
Barker Gibson; son; winder-on (cotton); aged 32; unmarried; born Walsden
Jackson Gibson; son; twister-in (cotton); aged 28; unmarried; born Walsden
Martha J. Turner; daughter; cotton weaver; aged 34; married; born Walsden
Annie Turner; grandchild; aged 2; born Littleborough

No. 91 Featherstall Road.

No mention is made of Martha's husband, however, as the census recorded the persons present in a household on the date of the census, Mr Turner may have been absent on business and not necessarily deceased. The early directories give the address as No. 91 Featherstall Road.

For some reason, many temporary licences were granted for this beerhouse in the period 1874 to 1877. This may have been a typical example of the type of beerhouse that the licensing authorities sought to close down at the start of the twentieth-century. Certainly its licence was not renewed in 1907 and earlier that year, the *Rochdale Observer* of 9 February, reported objections to the Musicians Arms continuing as a licensed public house.

LIST OF LICENSEES:

1872	Mary Whittaker	1878-1879	David Spencer
1872-1874	Samuel Baker	1879-1884	Enoch Gibson
1874	James Baker	1884	Agnes Hargreaves
1874-1876	Edwin Brearley	1884-1885	Tom Taylor
1876-1877	James Lord	1885-1886	Edwin Brearley
1877	Thomas Brearley	1886-1887	Abraham Fletcher
1877	Joseph Walmsley	1887-1899	Robert Halstead

NEW INN

As early as 1823, this inn was known as the Colliers Arms *(q.v.)*. It is suspected that the name was changed when some rebuilding took place in the 1870s.

Standing, as it does, at the bottom of Arm Road, it was no doubt frequented by the workers from the Dearnley Colliery and Starring Potteries. The windows of the pub have some of the original glazing that depicts the brewery logo.

The only additional record that we have been able to obtain is that of a prosecution of the landlord, Thomas Clegg, on 19 February 1859, for drinking after hours on a Sunday. He was fined five shillings.

LIST OF LICENSEES:

1823-1832	James Chadwick	1923-1931	Clarence Thomas
1843-1852	Robert Buckley	1931-1933	Andrew John Kilpatrick
1857-1862	Thomas Clegg	1933-1937	James Thwaite
1872	John Barlow	1937-1954	George Arthur Pate
1872-1876	Joseph Butterworth	1954-1955	Ronald Duckworth
1876-1886	Rachel Butterworth	1955-1961	John Grimes Heap
1886-1890	William Howarth	1961-1978	Edward Levi Rigg
1890	William H. Eddhouse	1978-1984	Phyllis Rigg
1890	John Cryer	1984-1991	John Richard Whittaker
1890-1891	Ann Cryer	1991	Gaynor Ramsden
1891-1893	William Dugdale	1991-1993	Annie Marie Howarth
1893-1894	Samuel Dawson	1993	Roy Butler
1895-1902	James Wrigley	1993-1995	Alexander Nicol
1902-1909	Alice Wrigley	1995-1996	Anthony Devanney

 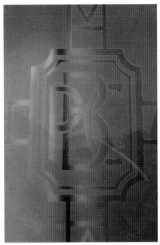

Above left: The New Inn, formerly the Colliers Arms.

Above right: Glazing still to be seen in the pub windows, depicting an old brewery logo.

1909-1911	Martin Murray	1996	Terence Blackshaw
1911-1914	William Howarth	1996-2001	Trish Susan Marshall
1914-1917	George Leach	2001-2002	Trish Susan Kershaw
1917-1918	Elizabeth Taylor	2002-2005	Alison Jane Bamford
1918-1923	Thomas Spencer Ogden		

OX AND PLOUGH

This is the first pub situated on the way into Littleborough from Rochdale.

Little history is recorded of this public house. The Rochdale Star reports an application for a licence granted to John Rothwell in 1889 for the sale of wine for consumption on or off the premises.

In its latter years, this public house has seen an array of short-term licensees.

LIST OF LICENSEES:

1872-1876	Rachael Butterworth	1970-1987	Robert Dearden
1876-1883	John Marsden	1987-1991	Vera Dearden
1883-1887	Martin Marsden	1991-1993	Ann Marie Cook
1887-1889	Robert William Greenwood	1993-1994	Lee Anthony Armstrong
1889-1897	John Thomas Rothwell	1994-1996	Michael Wayne Diggle
1897-1898	John Andrew Harwood	1996-1997	Lesley Atkinson
1898-1902	Ralph Mellor	1997	Anthony Wayne Diggle
1904-1905	John William Dawson	1997	Deborah Marsden
1905-1907	John Walker Allen	1997-1998	Martin Francis Holland
1907-1908	Henry Nuttall	1998	Margaret O'Mara

Left: The Ox and Plough with the tower of Birch Hill, former workhouse, in the background.

Below: A photograph of one of the Rochdale Corporation Water Work's 'navvies' outside the Ox and Plough; (Paul Quinn.)

1908-1916	Arthur Gorton	1998-1999	Leslie Edward Riley
1916-1925	James Murray Crossley	1999	Deirdre Ann Moore
1925-1935	Mary Crossley	1999-2002	Anthony Philip Dale
1935-1943	George Leach	2002-2003	Gillian Josephine Armitage
1943-1944	Anne Leach	2003	David P N Butterworth
1944-1945	John Stock	June 2003	Numerous Licensees
1945-1956	Robert James Caldwell	2003-2004	Elizabeth Margaret Ferguson
1956-1957	John Lavin	2004	Mandy Cryer
1957-1964	Fred England	2004	John Patrick O'Shea
1964-1965	William Robinson Bowdler	2004-2005	Linda Maria Rowbotham
1965-1970	Frank Greenwood		

PARKHILL HOUSE

A house of uncertain date situated at Lower Shore and bought from John Schofield of Stubley by Hugh Tate, who had been licensee since at least 1872. This house, with its associated gardens, known locally as the 'Rhubarb Patch' was owned by the grandson of Hugh into the 1980s and at that time still retained some of the features of its pub days.

Harold Tate, grandson to Hugh Tate, told the society of the 'beer allowance' to Cleggs Mill, mentioned in the introductory notes. He also mentioned that one of the outhouses was used as a brewhouse. The following quote from *Rastrick Industrial Archaeology* may give some indication of the contents of similar outhouses in this area:

> In the small public house, the country house and even some town houses, the brewhouse was no more than a range of cellars, or more commonly a group of outhouses in the yard. The apparatus in these included tubs, a copper for boiling sufficient water and a store for barrels.

It was here that some of these old utensils mentioned in the introductory notes have been seen by the society.

Some indication of the independence shown by the people of Littleborough can perhaps be seen from the following quote out of the licensing records: 'Why Rice Tate's name on the May renewal of licence?' It would, after all, be obvious to anyone from Littleborough, that Rice should follow his father Hugh into possession, just as his son, Harold, should follow Rice. The house officially ceased to function as an inn on the 7 January 1942.

Rhubarb from the Tate's gardens was bottled by local producers, Beswick's Pickles. The Tates were recorded as market gardeners as early as 1856.

The house is now a private dwelling and is situated on the opposite side of Shore Road from the King William IV and is bounded on one side by the public footpath that goes from Lower Shore to Starring, alongside the famous rhubarb gardens.

LIST OF LICENSEES:

1872-1889	Hugh Tate
1889-1938	Rice Tate
1938-1942	Harold Tate

Harold Tate playing 'Knurr and Spell' outside Parkhill House in the 1930s.

Starring, from Lower Shore – looking across the famous Tate Rhubarb Gardens.

Parkhill House today, a private dwelling.

PUNCHBOWL INN

Although this inn closed in 1908, the inn sign was still in existence in 1926, when the following article by A.R. appeared in the *Rochdale Observer*:

> The sign of a punch bowl on a house at Summit (Littleborough), suggests to the modern mind, merely conviviality and an old time drink which has left its name in the literature. But hear what the historian has to say: "The Punch Bowl was first introduced into signs at the end of the seventeenth century, when punch became the fashionable drink. Punch became the Whigg drink, whilst the Tories adhered to sack, claret and canary, connected in their memory with bygone times and things. Hence, the Punch Bowl was added as a kind of party badge to many of the Whigg tavern signs.
>
> At election times, public houses were used as candidates committee rooms and on polling day as convenient places where voters of the opposite party might be 'bottled'. This was one way of dealing with electors likely to poll on the opposite side, the idea being to ply them with beer and hold them captive until polling was finished and it was too late for them to vote."

The hanging bracket for this sign was still outside the door of the house at Summit in the 1980s, in a row of three that are mentioned in the 1861 census in the following manner:

1 Punchbowl Inn; Joseph Travis; grocer and beerseller
2 Punchbowl Inn; George Walsh; winder
3 Punchbowl Inn; Blacksmiths and wheelwrights shop

The 1881 census records:

Punch Bowl
Peter Ormerod; head; beerseller; aged 52; born Holmes Chapel
Ann Ormerod; wife; aged 42; born Brown Birk, Lancashire
Alice A. Ormerod; daughter; cotton weaver; aged 12; born Cornholme
Thomas H. Ormerod; son; cotton warehouse boy; aged 10; born Todmorden
Ada Ormerod; daughter; cotton weaver; aged 5; born Wardle
Frank Ormerod; son; cotton weaver; aged 4; born Wardle
Mary E. Ormerod; daughter; cotton weaver; aged 8 months; born Calderbrook
Samuel Shepherd; boarder; cotton factory engineer; aged 48; married; born Rochdale
George Fitton; boarder; cotton cardroom jobber; aged 20; unmarried; born Congleton

The references to the youngest three children being cotton weavers suggests that in this household, they started young or their careers were mapped out well in advance. The 1891 census records, 'Thomas Cryer; head; male; aged 39; beamer and beerhouse keeper; born Bacup, Lancashire.'

The Punchbowl closed its doors in 1908, following objections to renewal of the licence first recorded in the *Rochdale Observer* of 9 February 1907, thus:

> The Punch Bowl. Mr J.T. Worth appeared for John Bulcock of Todmorden, the owner of the Punch Bowl beerhouse, Summit. Inspector Purvis said the house was licensed prior to 1869. Mr Worth remarked that the present tenant was a manageress. He did not think that the closing of the house would cause much inconvenience to anybody.

Sladen Wood Mill at Rock Nook, one of the mills whose workers were catered for by the numerous beer-houses and inns on this stretch of Todmorden Road.

The Punchbowl Inn as it stands today, at No. 22 Summit.

The building then came into the ownership of an Abraham Brierley, who applied to Littleborough Urban District Council in 1909 to convert the pub into two dwellings. This was refused but permission was subsequently granted for conversion and No. 22 Summit remains a private dwelling.

LIST OF LICENSEES:

1861	Joseph Travis	1883–1896	Thomas Cryer
1871	John Travis	1896	Sarah Cryer
1871	Welcome Roger	1896–1899	William Taylor
1871–1873	Peter Ormerod	1899–1902	David Whittaker
1873–1876	Joseph Stott	1902	William Heap
1876	Alfred Stevenson	1902–1906	Annie L Elizabeth Walker
1876–1879	John Cryer	1906–1907	Kate Foster
1879–1881	Peter Ormerod	1907–1908	Joseph Foster
1881	Jane Howarth		

QUEEN ANNE

The history of this inn, as has been previously mentioned, is bound with the history of Rochdale as a whole. The following quotation from Fishwick's *History of Rochdale Parish* will suffice to show its ancient connections, 'Close to the highway from Town House to Reddyshore Scout Gate, Richard Duerden built a house in the year 1610 which he called 'Warcock Hill', but subsequently changed to the more modern sounding title of 'Handle Hall.'

The present building is used as a public house with the sign of the Queen Anne. Over the door is engraved on a stone – '*1610 Richardus Dearden struxit; Jacobus Dearden de novo restitutet 1829*'

Following the elevation of the Dearden family as Lords of the Manor of Rochdale and their subsequent move from Littleborough, the house came into the tenancy of the Bamford family who appear to have been landlord or landlady on several occasions over the following 100 years. The date stone would suggest that ownership of the building remained with the Deaden family during this period.

The first recorded Bamford was a Thomas Bamford who was buried at Rochdale Graveyard following his death in 1759. His wife, Sarah, was also buried in Rochdale Graveyard after her death in 1770. Their son, also Thomas, died in 1785 and their daughter, Molly, died in 1790. Both were buried alongside their parents. The first Bamford to be recorded as a landlord was Thomas, grandson of Thomas Senior.

In 1856, a John Harris applied for transfer of licence from the current tenant, Joseph Howarth but the licence transfer was opposed as it was found that the new licensee had not paid the outgoing tenant and owed him £80 11s 1d; an offer of £40 was made but no record of acceptance has been found.

The 1881 census records:

Queen Ann Inn, 6 Handle Hall
Isabella Sutcliffe; head; landlady & farmer; aged 34; widow; born Wardle
John R. Sutcliffe; son; scholar; aged 8; born Wardle
Samuel Sutcliffe; son; scholar; aged 6; born Wardle
James Sutcliffe; son; scholar; aged 4; born Littleborough
Henry Laynd; brother; farm labourer; aged 22; unmarried; born Littleborough
Thomas Rawson; boarder; farm labourer; aged 35; born Eccles

LIST OF LICENSEES:

1818	Thomas Bamford	1872	Charles Bamford
1823	C Bamford	1872–1875	John Barlow
1824	Sarah Bamford	1875–1877	Robert Sutcliffe
1845	Charles Bamford	1877–1882	Isabella Sutcliffe
1851–1852	William Rigg	1882–1901	James Thomas Stott
1856	Joseph Howarth	1901–1905	John Edmund Singleton
1856	John Harris	1905–1910	George Hoyle
1858–1861	Henry Redmond	1910–1911	Thomas Roker
????	John Holt	1929–1932	James Law
1870	Esther Cryer	1932–1934	Louis Charles Wild
1870	William Bamford	1934	Martin Gumbley

Date stone of Handle Hall, indicating the date of construction and of rebuilding.

The Queen Anne, photographed, we think, in the 1860s. The landlord is a John Holt, but we have not been able to trace the years of his tenure.

Handle Hall and the Queen Anne as it stands today.

QUEENS HEAD

This was another name for the above pub at Handle Hall. Refer to the Queen Anne for a fuller history and details of the licensees.

QUEENS HOTEL, LITTLEBOROUGH

On one of the lintels of this house is to be seen the date 1861. This lintel above the door records the initials of Richard and Betty Durham and it is likely that Richard Durham was landlord from the date the pub opened in 1861. A report in the *Rochdale Observer* dated 30 January 1864 gives details of the enrolment of members of the newly formed Littleborough Provident Building Society. This report in the *Rochdale Observer* lists Richard Durham as landlord. The 1881 census records:

Queens Hotel, Church Street
Sarah Crossley; head; beerseller; widow; aged 54; born Walsden
Susannah Sutcliffe; daughter; unmarried; aged 23; born Rochdale
Sarah Jane Sutcliffe; daughter; unmarried; aged 20; born Manchester

One of the more interesting points that have come to light appears in an advertisement in the 1933 shopping guide, of which we include part:

Bottles reserved,
Mild and Bitter—the best.
Ask for '3B's'—splendid.
Bass, Worthington, Guinness.
Don't forget the Baby 'G'.
Port and Sherry—Bottles from 5/- to 9/-
QUALITY :: SERVICE :: CIVILITY

LIST OF LICENSEES:

1861-1872	Richard Durham	1923-1934	Norman Etchells
1872-1874	William Carter	1934-1942	Herbert Allen
1874-1875	Henry Clayton	1943-1955	Isaac James Rushton
1876	Joseph Hopkinson	1955-1958	Frank Fletcher
1876-1879	William Heap	1958-1960	Clarence Butterworth
1879-1880	William Webster	1960-1967	Archie Maurice Whitham
1880-1887	Sarah Crossley	1967-1969	Granville Painter
1887-1889	Josiah Wild	1969-1972	George Oakley
1889-1891	William Rhodes	1972-1982	John Cowen
1891-1895	Joseph Bullwright	1982-1984	John Payne
1895-1902	William Holden	1984-1987	Philip C Cram
1902-1903	John Cropper Taylor	1987-1989	Jean Creevy
1903-1911	William Holden	1989-1995	Susan Elizabeth McClure
1911-1915	William Grime	1995-2005	Stephen Hesford
1915-1923	Arthur Hollow		

The Queens Hotel, Littleborough; still a thriving public house.

QUEENS HOTEL, HOLLINGWORTH LAKE

Being one of the inns at Hollingworth Lake, this was one of those made popular in the rise of Victorian tourism in the 1870s. This is shown in the advertisements in *Worral's Directory* of 1873 in which the following are available: 'Good accommodation for pic-nic & other parties; good stabling.'

Martha Marland, the licensee of this establishment in the 1870s, possessed one of those names that are always associated with the lake and its environs.

The Queens Hotel was part of the Peanock Farm complex, on Peanock Lane, off Milnrow Road. The earliest record of a landlord is a report in the *Rochdale Observer* on 8 December 1866 of a creditors meeting in connection with Peanock Farm and the Queens Hotel in which Charles Buckley is referred to as landlord. On 5 January 1867 a 'sale by ticket' was advertised in the *Rochdale Observer* and the building appears to have been purchased by one Edward Hill, as he advertised the pub for let by private treaty in the *Rochdale Observer* on 23 February that year. The advertisement describes:

> The goodwill and possessions of and in the very valuable Hotel known as the Queen's Hotel, situate at Hollingworth Lake ... with the Pleasure Grounds belonging thereto, and late in the occupation of said Charles Buckley, together with the newly-erected pavilion, dancing stage, brewhouse, stabling, barn, shippon, and other outbuildings, with twenty acres of first-class meadow and pasture land.

> Hollingworth Lake is now the fashionable resort of thousands of people from the manufacturing

districts of Lancashire and Yorkshire; and the above Hotel, which is now replete with domestic conveniences, presents an opportunity which rarely occurs for an enterprising tenant, the house doing a first-class business and the late tenant having at a very great outlay [made] inside the premises commodious and comfortable, and now well adapted for carrying on a lucrative and extensive business which the premises will always command from visitors frequenting Hollingworth Lake at all seasons of the year.

A second advertisement placed in the *Rochdale Observer* on 23 February 1867, described the hotel thus:

> To be let by private treaty, the Queen's Hotel, Hollingworth Lake, near Rochdale. The house is now fitted up in first-class style, well adapted to carry on an extensive business, and contains two parlours, sitting-room, club-room, tap-room, bar, kitchen, three bedrooms, large attic, four ale, wine, and spirit cellars, office, wash and brew-house. Also stabling for six horses, with vacant land and shed for carriages &c. &c.; together with the newly-erected pavilion, dancing stage and pleasure grounds.

Martha Marland, who was recorded as owner, was more likely to have only been tenant, as the licence was transferred to her on 1 June 1867; she was likely to be the tenant who responded to Edward Hill's offer to let by treaty, noted above.

The *Rochdale Times* in January 1868 reported a case of after hours drinking at the Queens Hotel, Hollingworth Lake and it was found to be legal if those caught drinking could prove that they had travelled more than three miles to get to the pub.

LIST OF LICENSEES:

1866	Charles Buckley	1894	James Howarth
1867–1879	Martha Marland	1894–1910	Robert Wolstenholme
1879–1890	Charles Holt	1910–1911	Joseph Lees
1890	John Woodhead	1911–1912	Alfred Wellburn
1890–1893	Thomas Ramsden	1912–1915	John Thomas Taylor
1893–1894	Charles Hudson Baxter	1915–1923	Willie Collinge

RAILWAY HOTEL

Standing near Littleborough station, this is one of two railway pubs in the Littleborough area; the other having closed and reopened under another name.

The following reference is to be found in a rating list of 1890, 'Thomas Wild, Inghams; public house and stables; £40. 00s. 00d; self-occupier.' The Inghams mentioned refers to Inghams Lane, the side road in which the inn stands. The first record of a landlord goes back to 13 August 1870 when the farmer Thomas Wild of Inghams Farm built the hotel and applied for a full spirit licence. It is not recorded whether this application was successful, as three years later on 9 August 1873, the *Rochdale Observer* reported an application by the same Thomas Wild for a beer licence.

The pub changed its name at the end of the twentieth century to the Waterside before closing its doors in 2003 and reopening in 2004 as a restaurant, taking the last name of the pub.

The former Queens Hotel, on Peanock Lane at the side of Hollingworth Lake

LIST OF LICENSEES:

1870–1886	Thomas Wild	1945–1952	Charles Howarth
1886–1890	William Heap	1952–1963	John Thomas Kenny
1890–1895	Charles Stott	1963–1976	William Cunliffe Laycock
1895–1898	James Haigh	1976–1978	Robert Althrop
1898	Stansfield Gibson	1978–1981	Audrey Frances Hanning
1898–1899	Richard Blackburn	1981–1983	Joseph Watson
1899–1904	Harry Rigg	1983–1988	William Anthony Cooke
1904–1905	Robert Lord	1988	Colin Ratcliffe
1905–1906	Hamer Hollinrake	1988–1993	Eric Malcolm Howarth
1906–1914	Frederick Ingham	1993–1994	Clifford Lignum
1914–1916	Annie Ingham	1994–1995	Gerrard McCoy
1916–1930	John Richards	1995–1998	John Edward Grindrod
1930	Gerald Richards	1998–2004	Jeanette Schofield
1930–1945	Arthur Butterworth		

RAILWAY INN

This was the original name of the Tophams Tavern at Smithy Bridge. Refer to Tophams Tavern for a fuller history and details of the licensees.

The Waterside Restaurant, formerly the Railway Hotel.

RAKE INN

Another of Littleborough's coaching inns; this one is situated at the start of the climb up to Blackstone Edge on the old turnpike road. Although the earliest reference found is to Abraham Whitehead in 1734, it is obvious that the inn is much older and a date of 1695 has been suggested. This Abraham describes himself as, 'at the bottom of Windy Bank Rake, Ale House Keeper'.

The name of the inn has been the point of some controversy as to its origin, as this article in the *Rochdale Observer* of 1926 indicates:

> Asked for the derivation of the sign, a stranger might think that it had a haymaking origin, but such is not the case. It is obvious that the name comes from Rakewood, nearby ... the word Rake ... derives from the Anglo-Saxon word 'hraca', the throat or jaws, and has in the past been applied to a pit, a delph, or narrow pass. Anyone who notices the formation of the ground at Rakewood will see how applicable the name is in this case... The building has been an inn since 1696. A thorough inspection of the interior of the premises shows the building methods of that period, the floors and roofs are upheld by stout oaken beams – one might also say trees, for in most instances they have been very slightly and roughly dressed... in the corner of the living room some narrow windows pierce a wall some two feet thick.

This discussion on the name seems to be searching for a piece of history when in fact the inn was known as the Hayrake in 1832. This seems to be a more reasonable origin of the name.

It is reported that a ghost of a laughing cavalier appears to anyone called Anne who lives in the inn. This is found in the *Rochdale Observer* for 1967 when, 'Mrs Turton (Annie) reports seeing

The Rake Inn on Blackstone Edge Old Road.

him one morning towards the end of 1965, at about ten past three. She describes him as – a big fellow with a big round face and his big cavalier's hat held in front of him and wearing a lovely amber brooch.'

There appears to be some confusion as to the landlords of this public house in the mid to late 1800s. Licensing records place Edward Collingwood as landlord from 1861-1876. However, records of licence transfers published in local papers appear to indicate that whilst he commenced as landlord in 1861 and finally retired as landlord in 1876, some changes occurred in the early 1870s, at a time when it was likely that this Edward Collingwood became a bankrupt. This is borne out by a report in the *Rochdale Observer* of 15 July 1871 of a meeting of the creditors of said Edward Collingwood. By 1881, the census records:

Rake Inn
Elizabeth Hurst; head; licensed victualler; widow; aged 47; born in Wales
Farewell Hurst; son; fulling miller; unmarried; aged 19; born Littleborough
Mary Hurst; daughter; cotton operative; unmarried; aged 17; born Littleborough
Sarah Hurst; daughter; cotton operative; unmarried; aged 13; born Littleborough
Fanny Hurst; daughter; scholar; aged 9; born Littleborough
James Hurst; son; scholar; aged 5; born Littleborough
Thomas Hamlett; boarder; papermaker; unmarried; aged 32; born Stafford

A further example of public houses being used for inquests comes with a report in the *Rochdale Observer* of 1 September 1860 of a coroner's inquest at the Rake Inn into the deaths of three miners working at Gatehouse Colliery. Headed 'Fatal Colliery Accident at Littleborough', the report gives:

On Tuesday last, Mr Thomas Fferand Dearden, coroner, held an inquest at the Rake Inn, Littleborough, on the bodies of William Whipp, James Kershaw and Jacob Leach, colliers, who were accidentally killed at the Gatehouse and Rake Colliery, while descending the shaft to go to work about seven o'clock on Saturday morning – last. It appears that the shaft is 108 yards deep, and about 40 yards down is an old working. The shaft is too narrow for both cages to pass and re-pass except at one particular place opposite the old working. The cage that the three deceased and another youth named Jeffrey Lees, were in met the other cage at the right place, but from some mysterious cause the ascending cage overturned the descending cage and all four were thrown out. Lees had the good fortune to be pitched into the old working but the other three were thrown down the shaft and were completely smashed.

LIST OF LICENSEES:

1734	Abraham Whitehead	1913–1927	William Roker
1818–1824	James Clegg	1945–1953	Harold Mitchell
1832	Susanna Clegg	1953–1961	Nellie Mitchell
1843–1852	James Wild	1961–1968	Wilfred Turton
1858	Abraham Spencer	1968–1969	Annie Turton
1861–1876	Edward Collingwood	1969–1978	James Lawrence Gorse
1870	Henry Collingwood	1978–1981	Vincent Vernon Street
1870	Harriet Collingwood	1981–1982	Nigel Christopher Fox
1870	Ann Butterworth Collingwood	1982–1985	Andrew Alexander Wilson
1870	John Thomas Stott	1985	Colin Ratcliffe
1871	Harriet Collingwood	1985–1991	Peter Hughes
1876–1878	Edward Thistlewhite	1991	Harry Adshead
1878–1879	James Hurst	1991–2001	Gaynor Ramsden
1879–1887	Elizabeth Hurst	2001–2002	Mark Hadfield
1887–1890	John Beresford	2002	Andrea Daphne Sleaman
1890–1891	Joseph Heap	2002	Gary Michael Wood
1891–1895	Thomas Tuson	2002–2003	Joanna Aitchinson
1895–1910	William Fielden	2003	Michael Heaford
1910–1912	Eli Rothwell	2003–2005	Terance Heaton
1912–1913	Wally Wood		

RED LION

There was an inn in this area as early as 1626, but the earliest record of a landlord is in a report of the death of Richard Gibson, born 1720, who died on 15 December that year aged thirty-eight years and described as innkeeper, Littleborough. Another early reference of a licensee appears in the Turnpike Trust records for 1760-61, when, 'The Todmorden Turnpike Trust held four meetings at the sign of the Red Lion, the house of Mary Gibson.'

At one time the house was part of the Pike House properties of the Beswicke family as is reported in Travis' *Notes on Littleborough*:

Job Cogswell & Co. Boat Builders occupied the Red Lion … not as a public house or inn but for the accommodation of the men and the horses in their employment … they had to pay the licence so that Mr Beswicke, of Pike House, the owner, would not suffer loss by lapse of the same in the event of their giving up the premises.

Another early landlord was Robert Cogswell. Despite Travis' *Notes on Littleborough* describing the Cogswell tenure of the Red Lion as one of provision of accommodation for workers at their adjacent boat yard, on the death of Robert Cogswell in 1790 he was described as son of Job Cogswell, Littleborough, and innkeeper. By 1851 the census gives, 'Lower Ealees; Edmund Aspinall (41); publican and farmer of 12 acres; born Heywood.' In 1881, the census records:

Red Lion
Rachel Sutcliffe; head; licensed victualler; aged 48; widow; born Burnley
Sophie Lawson; cousin; servant; aged 46; unmarried; born Glasgow
Sarah Ellen Shore; servant; aged 16; unmarried; born Crewe

The many efforts by this and other Littleborough pubs in support of local and national charities is treated in the general introduction notes, but it is worth mentioning here that the Red Lion appears in the list of 1909 as giving a donation of 13s 1d to the local Poor Children's Treat.

The *Rochdale Observer* of 12 October 1861 records a meeting at the Red Lion of the shareholders of the Littleborough Manufacturing Co. Ltd, whereby share capital was increased to £100,000. The Littleborough Manufacturing Co. Ltd. built and operated Frankfort Mill on Halifax Road; indeed the *Rochdale Observer* of 16 November that year reports on the provision of a meal at the Red Lion for builders of Frankfort Mill. The landlord at that time was Edmund Aspinall, who continued as landlord until 1866 when he advertised in the *Rochdale Observer* on 12 May that year that the Red Lion was 'to let by ticket', describing the property as a public house, with farm lands and buildings.

The Red Lion and its ample surrounding courtyard was used as a place of auction in the 1800s, and perhaps even earlier. A notice in the *Rochdale Times* for 12 May 1883 gives:

Mr B. Consterdine is favoured with instructions from Mr Henry Maden, Littleborough, to sell by auction, on Wednesday May 16th 1883, in the yard adjoining the Red Lion Hotel, Littleborough, eight head of horned cattle, one cob, one pony and six pigs, *viz:-* One roan twinter for August, one ditto five weeks served, one ditto, one red ditto, one red cow for August, two ditto fresh in milk, one roaned ditto; one grey cob, five years old, 15-1 hands, very quiet and works all kinds of harness; one black pony, 12 hands; six store pigs. Notes and other particulars at time of sale. The Auctioneer can with confidence recommend the above as being first-class stock, and worthy of inspection to his numerous customers.

The *Rochdale Times* on 19 May 1883 reported the proceedings of an inquest held at the Red Lion by Rochdale Coroner, Mr Molesworth, into the case of Sarah Watterson who was found drowned in the Rochdale Canal at Ealees Wharf. It reports that the body of the deceased was 'lying at the Red Lion' during the inquest. Her husband was suffering from 'delirium tremens' during the inquest and confirmed that his wife had recently spent two years in Crumpsall Lunatic Asylum. The police felt that there were no grounds to suspect her husband of drowning her and the inquest heard from Harriet Brown of Victoria Terrace who said that the deceased had threatened to drown herself on several occasions. Verdict: suicide while of unsound mind.

The provision of meals at public houses for workers and paid for by their employers was something of a rarity in the 1800s, and these events tended to be reported in the local newspapers.

The Red Lion, popular meeting place and scene of many inquets held in Littleborough.

The *Rochdale Times* on 30 January 1886 reported that Charles Kershaw, Fuller and Dyer of Field Mill, laid on a meal for 100 hands at the Red Lion.

LIST OF LICENSEES:

1758	Richard Gibson	1931–1934	George Watkins
1760–1761	Mary Gibson	1934–1936	Edward Taylor
1790	Robert Cogswell	1936–1939	Mary Ann Moss
1843–1851	William Banks	1939–1940	Robert Catterall
1851–1866	Edmund Aspinall	1940–1942	Hilda Edwards
1867	James Brierley	1942–1944	William Rumney
1868	William Sutcliffe	1944–1953	Herbert Collins
1870	James Sutcliffe	1953–1956	James Knight Coutts
1872–1882	Rachel Sutcliffe	1956–1957	Brian Allen
1882	Eliza Lawson	1957–1959	John Chadwick
1882–1884	Frederick Lawson	1959–1964	Norman Park
1884–1904	John Edward Rowell	1964–1968	Walter Whitehurst
1904–1917	John Howarth	1968–1972	Joseph Thornton Beresford
1917–1918	Hamer Hollinrake	1972–1976	John Michael Doherty
1918–1919	Leah Hollinrake	1976–1981	Joseph Bodell
1919–1922	Hamer Hollinrake	1981–1982	David Robinson
1922–1927	John Joseph Grundy	1982–2005	David Russell Cocker
1927–1931	Harrison Gladwell		

ROCK TAVERN

Another Summit pub; described in the 1861 census as being at No. 3 Rock Nook. This no doubt was one of the beerhouses that became pubs in the 1870s.

The 1861 census records Elizabeth Kershaw (widow) as beerseller, aged sixty-nine. By licence transfer dated 19 August 1871, Joseph Stott became landlord, taking over from Thomas Law. When Thomas Law became landlord is not recorded.

The 1881 census records:

Rock Nook
William H. Sutclife; head; beer seller; aged 34; born Todmorden
Frances Sutcliffe; wife; aged 38; born Stockport
Ann Mather; sister-in-law; cotton weaver; aged 40; unmarried; born Stockport
Thomas Heap; lodger; brick maker; aged 20; unmarried; born Manchester
John Wood; lodger; carter; aged 30; unmarried; born Manchester

The 1891 census records Frances Sutcliffe, now widowed, as beerhouse keeper, aged fifty-five. The discrepancy in age between her entry in the 1881 census and 1891 census is common of the errors found in census returns for that period.

LIST OF LICENSEES:

1861	Elizabeth Kershaw	1879-1887	William Henry Sutcliffe
1871	Thomas Law	1887-1903	Frances Sutcliffe
1871	Joseph Stott	1903	Ann Mather
1872-1873	James Greenwood	1903-1911	John William Redman
1873-1875	Jonathon Higham	1911-1912	John William Dawson
1875	Ann Higham	1912-1915	William Albert Crossley
1875-1877	James Whitehead	1915	Greenwood Hargreaves
1877-1879	John Crowther		

Rock Nook, houses lining the side of the valley on Todmorden Road.

Fothergill & Harvey's Rock Nook Mill, another mill whose workers sought refreshment at one of the many beer-houses and public houses in the immediate vicinity.

Regulars lined up outside the pub with Greenwood Hargreaves, the last landlord.

Rock Tavern as it stands today, converted into a private dwelling.

ROYAL EXCHANGE

At the junction of Featherstall and Whitelees Roads, this inn was advertised in the trades directories for 1894 as being owned by Calvert Yates, beer and wine seller and professional cricketer.

The earliest reference to a landlord is that of William Rickell in 1869. The following year, a record of the licence transfer exists between William Rickell and Ann Smith.

LIST OF LICENSEES:

1869–1870	William Rickell	1935–1938	Ronald Mitchell
1870	Ann Smith	1938–1948	Frank Taylor
1872	Thomas Schofield	1948–1949	Wallace Acton
1872–1876	Robert Brearley	1949–1951	James Norman Duffin
1876–1877	Luke Howarth	1951–1955	Harold Chambers
1877–1885	John Wesley Barker	1955–1956	Edith Chambers
1885–1886	William Heap	1956–1957	John Bowdler
1886–1894	Calvert Yates	1957–1960	Joseph Hardman
1903	Harry Cocker	1960–1964	William Robinson Bowdler
1903–1904	Handel Farrow	1964–1971	Thomas Cochrane Drummond
1904–1905	James Hirst	1971–1976	Arthur Frederick Hartley
1905–1907	Aaron Keeble	1976–1979	Joseph Lamb
1907–1911	Nancy Keeble	1979–1982	James Phillip Hughes
1911	Nancy Durham	1982–1984	Godfrey I Higginbotham
1911–1913	William Fletcher	1984–1988	Malcolm Beswick
1913–1917	John Jas Fletcher	1988–1990	Ronald Hesling
1917–1933	Fred Helliwell	1990–2005	Craig Burrill
1933–1935	George Schofield		

ROYAL OAK, LITTLEBOROUGH

Another eighteenth-century pub in the centre of Littleborough that possibly served as a coaching house; the barn of which was replaced with the Queens Cinema. The earliest reference to this house gives an interesting insight into the economy of the nineteenth century, as we can see from this church notice of 1819:

> The taxpayers in the Township of Blatchinworth and Calderbrook are requested to take notice that a meeting will be held at the house of George Taylor, sign of The Royal Oak, Littleborough … for the purpose of laying a double rate for the year 1819.
>
> And also for rating a new erection, now inhabited … for and towards the necessary relief of the poor.

This rate was, in fact, assessed at 6s in the pound, amounting to £325 11s 1d.

In 1857, Edwin Waugh describes the inn as the one in which the most famous of dialect writers, Tim Bobbin, based his tale of Thomas and Mary. He also says that on Saturday nights and Fair days and Holydays, the inn would be crammed with villagers and neighbours from the surrounding hillsides. Inside would be, 'The clatter of pots and hunting cries, the thundering hurly burly of drunken anger or broken furniture, mingling with the boisterous tones of drunken fun.'

Workers taking up tramlines outside the Royal Exchange. Shops that once stood on the opposite corner of Whitelees Road are visible in the background.

The Royal Exchange public house on the junction of Featherstall Road and Whitelees Road.

The food requirements of the inn, at this time, would probably have been provided by the landlord who would have been, in the true sense of the word, a victualler. In his *Notes on Littleborough*, Travis describes the large holdings of the inn in the following manner:

The Royal Oak farm land then (1833) went by the bank of the River Roach to Featherstall Water and round by Whitelees to Hare Hill Mill and includes the James-hill and Will-hill, the barn and shippon standing on the top of James-hill, the road to them going up behind the public house.

By 1851, the inn was in the possession of, James Cryer; aged 60; victualler and farmer; Rachel Cryer; aged 63; his wife.

As late as 1874, James Stevenson, the landlord, was advertising 'good stabling', and this 'refuelling of transport' was continued into the middle of the last century with petrol pumps which used to be sited in front of the steps at the Oak and in the ownership of a garage that used to stand opposite the pub.

In 1858 we find Richard Durham as landlord. His tenure came to an end in 1861 when he and his wife had built the Queens Hotel on land adjacent to the Royal Oak, further along Church Street, as detailed in the entry for that public house.

In 1876 the Royal Oak Benefit (Building) Society was formed and the *Rochdale Observer* of 15 April that year gives details of the directors. The 1881 census records:

Oak Inn, Church Street
William Iddon; head; innkeeper and farmer of 14 acres; aged 40; born Crosston, Lancashire
Alice Iddon; wife; aged 33; born Preston
Elizabeth Iddon; daughter; aged 4; born Waterfoot
Alice Iddon; daughter; aged 3; born Waterfoot
Mary Iddon; daughter; aged 8 months; born Littleborough
Betsy Higinson; general domestic servant; widowed; aged 30; born Todmorden

LIST OF LICENSEES:

1818-1824	George Taylor	1920-1921	Joseph Shepherd
1843-1852	James Cryer	1921-1934	Walter Whipp
1858-1861	Richard Durham	1934-1936	Joseph Buckley
1867	Jonathon Mills	1936	Clara Walker
1869-1874	John Lowe	1936-1941	David Walker
1874-1875	Jonathon Mills	1941-1944	Albert William Brown
1875-1876	Thomas Greenwood	1944-1956	Harold Fitch
1876-1879	Esther Greenwood	1956-1967	William Henry Taylor
1879-1884	William Iddon	1967-1975	Joseph Anthony Waring
1884-1887	James Lord	1975-1984	John Michael McCreadie
1887-1888	Stephen Clough	1984-1985	Michael Kevin Ferguson
1888-1890	Anne Elizabeth Clough	1985-1991	Phillip Barrington Smith
1890-1892	Daniel Berry	1991-1992	Anthony Douglas Hutton
1892-1893	James Lord	1992-1998	Kenneth Brown
1893-1900	James Stephenson	1998-1999	June Richardson
1900-1913	Andrew Smith	1999-2001	Brian Richardson
1913-1918	George Bottomley	2001-2002	Martin James Brereton
1918-1920	Elizabeth Collier	2002-2005	Graham Martaine Wilde

The Royal Oak, Littleborough, photographed in 1975.

The Royal Oak, Littleborough as it stands today, one of several popular village-centre pubs.

ROYAL OAK, SMITHY BRIDGE

At Three Lane Ends, where the road turns to Milnrow, this was one of a group of cottages that are mentioned in an 1880 rating list, as follows, 'Daniel Spencer; Three Lane Ends; Public House; Gross rental £30; Self owner; Sarah Nuttall and others; Occupiers; £15 10s 0d.'

The licence expired in 1924; we are uncertain about when it was demolished. However, the society's current treasurer, Dilys Pearson, recalls the properties being occupied in the late 1940s/early 1950s; demolition taking place in the late 1950s/early 1960s. One of the cottages remains at the junction of 'three lane ends'

The *Rochdale Observer* of 31 May 1924 reports a court case between the last landlord and the penultimate landlord, George Ashworth and Joseph Smith, respectively:

'A Gamble on Seven'; The Sale of a Smithy Bridge Inn; Alleged Misrepresentation; Damages £800 for Purchaser, the report goes on to say:

The story of the sale of a Smithy Bridge beerhouse which was supposed to sell seven or eight half-barrels of beer per week was related at the Manchester Assizes, when Mr Justice Acton, sitting without jury, on Wednesday, dealt with an action by George Albert Ashwork of the Royal Oak Inn, Smithy Bridge, to recover damages from Joseph Smith for alleged misrepresentation in regard to the sale of that inn.

The plaintiff … arranged to purchase the inn for £1,600, with the stock and fixtures at a valuation. He alleged that the representation made to him as to the business done was that it amounted to seven or eight half-barrels per week, whereas the sales had turned out to be only about half that amount. The defendant denied that he made the representation alleged.

In opening the case, [it was] said the plaintiff was a man getting on in years … He thought he would like to get a little off-licence and having seen an advertisement in one of the Manchester newspapers he got into touch with a Mr Day, a business transfer agent, of Manchester. Eventually the plaintiff started out to see an off-licence business in Gorton. He went to Gorton by tramcar and whilst he was on the car a peculiar incident occurred. The plaintiff was asking the tramcar conductor the whereabouts of the off-licence at Gorton when a stranger engaged him (the plaintiff) in conversation. The stranger then said that his name was Bayliss and that he was a partner with the Mr Day previously mentioned. He informed plaintiff that the off-licence for the premises at Gorton had then been taken away and added 'why not go for a public house?' The plaintiff replied that he had not enough money for that, whereupon Mr Bayliss said 'we have got a public house near Rochdale doing a good trade and also some catering'. Ultimately plaintiff and Mr Bayliss went together to Smithy Bridge … As they were walking together along Smithy Bridge Road they passed a licensed house and Mr Bayliss said that the licence of that hotel was to be taken away, which would benefit the trade at the Royal Oak Inn. At the latter inn, the plaintiff was introduced to the landlord, Mr Smith, the defendant, who said that the trade of the house was 'seven or eight eighteens' (half-barrels) and added 'I gamble on seven regularly.'

When asked about records of the trade done, the defendant replied: 'We do not keep any books.'

The plaintiff had not been long at the inn before he realised the business of the house was not anything like what it had been represented as being. On one occasion the defendant went to the house and the plaintiff mentioned the matter to him but he replied: 'When the weather gets better it will be perfectly all right.' [The plaintiff's counsel remarked] 'It is rather problematical having to wait on Manchester weather for good trade.' (laughter).

The report goes on to reveal the true state of the inn's books when it was previously sold to the defendant in 1920. The other hotel referred to by the Mr Bayliss as, 'shortly to have its licence removed' was the Blue Ball, another untruth as the licence of the Blue Ball was not removed and continues to this day under the auspices of the 'Smithy Bridge'.

LIST OF LICENSEES:

1872–1879	Enoch Gibson	1915–1917	Edwin Stansfield
1879–1885	Daniel Spencer	1917–1919	Elizabeth Alice Stansfield
1885	Joseph William Morton	1919–1921	Edwin Stansfield
1885–1890	Ashworth Greenwood	1921–1922	Joseph Smith
1890–1891	Alice Greenwood	1922–1924	George Albert Ashworth
1891–1915	Thomas Smith		

The Royal Oak, at the junction of Smithy Bridge Road and Milnrow Road.

The remaining cottage, one of several that were attached to the Royal Oak at Smithy Bridge.

Smithy Bridge, nestling between the Manchester to Leeds Railway and the popular tourist attraction of Hollingworth Lake.

ROYAL OAK, SUMMIT

This was the original name of the Huntsman at Summit. Refer to Huntsman for a fuller history and details of the licensees.

SEVEN STARS

There is only one reference to this inn at Schofield Hall and that is in the directory for 1832. It is likely that this was simply a beerhouse serving the workers of the mills at Rakewood.

LIST OF LICENSEES:

1832   Jas Henthorn

SHEPHERDS REST / SHEPHERDS TAVERN

This house, on the newer of the Blackstone Edge roads, has had a number of names since it was first mentioned in the 1851 census:

1851 Fence Nook
1872 Shepherds Tavern
1889 Shepherds Rest Tavern

Remains of Schofield Hall and its various farm and mill buildings.

View of Hollingworth Lake from the site of Schofield Hall.

In 1906, the licence was refused, but allowed on appeal. The licence fully expired in 1915. The pub eventually became a transport cafe as can be seen, for example, in the trades directory for 1954, when C.P. Jenkins was given as having a transport cafe at No.1, Fence Nook.

The pub later became a restaurant (The Nook) and in 2005 the building was refurbished and converted into private dwellings.

The origins of the building may be revealed in details published on 18 May 1895 of an auction of the Shepherd Rest beerhouse, where it is stated that the lease was dated 1 November 1839. Originally a beerhouse, James Roberts, landlord in 1889, applied for a licence to sell wine. The beerhouse was purchased from James Roberts at the aforementioned auction by a Henry Harrison Whitney; his tenure lasted less than a year and an inquest into his death at the age of thirty-five was published in the *Rochdale Times* on 8 January 1896, thus:

> Littleborough. Sudden Death of a Publican. Mr Molesworth, county coroner, held a preliminary enquiry on Monday morning on the body of Henry Harrison Whitney, Shepherd's Rest, 1 Fence Nook, Littleborough, 35 years of age. Deceased had been subject to rheumatics since he was 17 years of age, but had never been medically attended. About 11.30 p.m. on Saturday he was assisted to bed by his wife and her brother, John Harrison McCormack, and frequently during the night he asked for a drink, which was given him. Shortly before five o'clock his wife noticed deceased looked worse, and, becoming alarmed, she sent her brother for the doctor, but on his arrival deceased expired.

In 1900, Edward Astin became landlord. His tenure was also very short lived and he died, according to the *Annals of Todmorden*, on 27 February that year, whilst in his forty-ninth year.

The Shepherds Rest photographed in the early 1900s; we think that the young lad with the bicycle was the landlady's son who was killed in the trenches during the First World War.

The Shepherds Rest today, newly converted into two dwellings.

He was buried at Christ Church, Todmorden. The annals record that he was until January 1900, pointsman at Walsden for the Lancashire & Yorkshire Railway Co., being in the service of the railway company for twenty-two years. His widow became licensee on his death but within the year had married Abraham Dearden and the licence transferred to him in 1901.

LIST OF LICENSEES:

1851	Abraham Spencer	1888–1895	James Roberts
1861	James Chadwick	1895–1896	Henry Harrison Whitney
1870	Charles Mitchell	1896–1898	John Patterson
1871	Robert Higham	1898–1900	Sutcliffe Kershaw
1872–1873	Jonathon Higham	1900	Edward Astin
1873–1876	John Greenwood	1900	Hannah Astin
1876–1882	William Whiteley	1900	Hannah Dearden
1882–1888	Thomas Rumney	1900–1901	Abraham Dearden
1888	Ann Rothwell	1901–1915	James Palfreyman

SLOOP INN

It has been previously given that The Sloop Tavern was at Durn. It is first found in the directories for 1823. A second mention was when the Overseers of the Poor met at the house of William Banks, sign of the Sloop, in 1825, to lay a rate for the relief of the poor.

It has been previously considered that the inn closed in about 1843, when William Banks transferred to the Red Lion and was widely believed that this pub was opened at the time when the Red Lion was used by Cogswell's boat builders.

This belief that the Sloop may have been connected with occupancy of the Red Lion by the Cogswell Boat Building Co. is not necessarily correct. During Cogswell's occupation of the Red Lion, we know that the licence for that inn was maintained and upon the death of Job Cogswell's son, his occupation was described as innkeeper. In addition, the Cogswell occupation of the Red Lion was predominantly in the late 1700s. It is more likely that this was simply a beerhouse at Durn that served the growing number of workers, at mills such as Frankfort (on Halifax Road) and those of the Law family at Durn.

Similarly, in an indenture dated 10 November 1846, being a settlement of marriage between Lawrence Henry Peel and Catherine Maria de Winton (after whom Peel Street and Winton Street in the town are respectively named), the Sloop is mentioned thus: 'and also that Messuage … used as an Inn or Public House formerly called by the sign of the Wheatsheaf but now of the Sloop Tavern … with Brew House, Butcher's Shop, barn, stable … late in the tenure of James Hurst and William Banks. Now in the occupation of Robert Hurst.'

This would place the Sloop Inn in the area of the Wheat Sheaf, Littleborough Square. The dates fit. Robert Hurst was licensee of the Wheat Sheaf from 1843 to 1866 and was responsible for its rebuilding in the 1860s, if Travis is to be believed.

LIST OF LICENSEES:

1823–1843   William Banks

SMITHY BRIDGE

This is the current name of the former New Blue Ball, a 1964 reincarnation of the old Blue Ball near to the railway level crossing on Smithy Bridge Road. Refer to the Blue Ball for a fuller history and details of the licensees.

SPORTSMANS REST

The name of the pub changed from the Dog & Partridge to the Sportsmans on 18 August 1989. In the 1980s there had been a stabbing incident at the pub and for a while thereafter, the pub was known locally as the Dog & Dagger.

See the Dog & Partridge for a fuller history.

LIST OF LICENSEES:

1872-1873	John Ashworth	1956-1958	Lawrence Garside
1873-1878	Samuel Jackson	1958-1960	Cecil Besant
1880-1884	Joshua Firth	1960-1961	Charles William Jones
1884-1887	James Marshall	1961-1962	Thomas Rothwell
1887	James Barlow	1962-1964	James Thomas Whipp
1887-1888	John Bamforth	1964	Charles Cormack
1888-1890	Mary Bamforth	1964-1966	Harold Evans
1890-1901	Sarah Firth	1966	Frank Watsonv
1901-1902	John William Howarth	1966-1982	Doris Ann Anchor
1902-1904	Joseph Lee	1982-1983	Brian Whitehead
1904-1906	Thomas Whittaker	1983-1984	Anthony Joseph Padlolli
1906-1907	Joseph Alfred Whittaker	1984-1985	Lilian Seirei
1907-1909	Joseph Cockcroft	1985-1987	Bernard Snee
1909-1926	Grace Cockcroft	1987-1988	Marilyn Patricia Molyneux
1926-1934	Welcome Fielden	1988-1989	Harry Arthur Bamber
1934-1935	Thomas Sutcliffe	1989-1992	Terence Sylvester Howarth
1935-1937	Samuel Lord	1992-1993	Catherine S. M. Howlett
1937-1943	Sarah Ann Hodkinson	1993	Barbara Cooke
1943-1947	Charles Hill	1993	Karen Montgomery
1947-1950	Samuel Lord	1993-1994	Anne-Marie Howarth
1950-1952	John Whittaker	1994-1997	Gregory George Bolton
1952-1955	George Southworth	1997	Peter John Drummond
1955	Paul Marsh	1997-2005	Michael John Fearon
1955	Ann Marsh	2005-	Paul Quinn

STAR HOTEL

We have been unable to ascertain when this hotel was first licensed. The first mention in the official records is for 1872. There are, however, references in the parish churchyard to William Wilson of Cleggswood Stars in 1848 and to John and Ann Whitworth in 1869 and their two

The Smithy Bridge, formerly the
New Blue Ball.

The Sportsmans Rest, one of
many public houses on Todmorden
Road between Littleborough and
Summit.

Inside the Sportsmans Rest with
the current landlord, Paul Quinn,
in 2006.

The former Star Hotel on Hollingworth Road.

daughters in 1853 and 1856. The first record of a landlord is in a notice of an auction of furniture in the *Rochdale Observer* for 7 September 1867.

By 1873 the hotel was advertising in *Worral's* Directory, 'Star Hotel; Hollingworth; John Woods, Proprietor; Tea, Coffee &c.; Apartments can be had; Good stabling'.

A taste of the attractions to be offered at the Lake can be seen in the *Rochdale Observer* advertisement of 1879, 'To be seen alive – a dog with five legs; at the house of Joseph Shepherd; Star Hotel, Hollingworth Lake.'

On 1 May 1879 there was an attempted murder at Hollingworth Lake. A Mrs Nuttall and her son, who were lodging at the Star Hotel, met her estranged husband, Isaiah Nuttall on the lake bank near to the Fishermans Inn. Isaiah Nuttall took hold of the child and threw him into the lake. Mrs Nuttall followed, in an attempt to save her child and was joined by her estranged husband, who proceeded to attempt to drown both wife and child. Mrs Nuttall resisted and was able to escape her husband and get both herself and her child out of the lake. Isaiah Nuttall drowned before he could be rescued from the water.

In the rating list of 1880, we find John Normanton to be the tenant, whilst Thistlewhites of Todmorden were the owners, the rental value being £25.

The hotel closed in January 1942. In the 1980s the building was refurbished and converted into a private dwelling.

LIST OF LICENSEES:

1867–1869	James Brierley	1894–1896	William Jackson
1870	Ann Butterworth Stott	1896–1899	Fielden Law
1870–1871	Isabella Allen	1899	John Chadwick
1871	John Woods	1899–1901	Daniel Garside
1871–1878	John Lord	1901	William Heap
1878–1879	Joseph Shepherd	1901–1903	Herbert Eastwood
1879–1883	John Normanton	1903–1904	William Blatherwick

1883–1884	George Harris	1904–1909	James Thomas Stott
1884–1887	Enoch Gibson	1909–1916	Radcliffe Brearley
1887–1888	Stephen Howarth	1916–1928	Luke Earnshaw
1888–1890	John Embley Gibson	1928–1930	Arthur Butterworth
1890–1894	Joseph Cryer	1930–1942	Edward Carter

STUBLEY OLD HALL

This was both a relatively new and relatively short lived public house opened at Stubley Old Hall, off Featherstall Road in 1987. Initially opened as a public house and hotel, it later became a public house and restaurant before closing at the turn of the century and subsequently has reverted back into a private dwelling.

The initial licence for the pub was by way of special removal from the White House on Lord Street in Rochdale.

LIST OF LICENSEES:

1987–1988	Mario Anreotti	1996–1997	Christopher John Walker
1988–1990	Graham John Walton	1997–1999	Peter Anthony Garner
1990–1992	John Turfrey	1999	Gary Steventon
1992	Andrew Kelly	1999	Phillip Anthony Gates
1992–1996	John Mark Turfrey	1999	Lynda May Lloyd

Featherstall Road from Dearnley towards Littleborough centre.

Stubley Old Hall, once more a private dwelling.

SUMMIT INN

James Lord is described, in 1818, as a victualler and butcher at Dog Hills. This would be the public house known as the Bull and Butcher on Calderbrook Road. It appears that this pub was pulled down to help build the Summit Inn, sometime in the 1820s: the stone being carried down the track past Wilmers. James Lord was born in 1790 and died in 1869. He was Littleborough's longest serving landlord. The Summit Inn was built when the new turnpike road was made to pass along the valley bottom from Littleborough to Todmorden. It is likely that this inn was used by canal and coach travellers as a suitable break in their journey.

The 1851 census gives:

Summit Inn
James Lord; victualler, butcher; aged 60
Sarah Lord; wife (58)
Thomas Lord; Son; commercial traveller (31)
Harriet Lord; daughter (26)
Emma Lord; daughter (17)
John Greenwood; servant (24)
Maria Asheton; servant (20)

The 1861 census gives, 'Summit Inn, Thomas Norris; head; male; aged 26; inn keeper; born Rochdale, Lancashire.'

In 1870 the Summit Inn was leased from John Holden by one James Tetlow, brother to John Tetlow of Tetlow's Sanitary Tube Works at Punchbowl Lock, Rock Nook. On 19 January 1878 the *Rochdale Observer* reported that he had hosted his brother's company's twentiety annual dinner for fifty people. The 1881 census gives:

Summit Inn
James Tetlow; head; publican; aged 59; born Castleton
Mary Tetlow; wife; aged 45; born Skipton
Jane Hunt; servant; aged 62; married; born Hanley Castle, Worcester
Edmund Crossley; farm servant; aged 58; unmarried; born Calderbrook

The *Rochdale Observer* reported on 23 May 1885 the death of the landlord's wife, Mary Tetlow; citing drunkenness and having been regularly beaten by her husband. An example of the use of this public house as venues for inquests is reported in the *Rochdale Observer* for 30 December 1882. Headlined 'Fatal Explosion at Steanor Bottoms' the report gives:

On Thursday morning, Mr Molesworth held an adjourned inquest at the Summit Inn near Littleborough concerning the death of Thomas Stansfield and James Thomas Ogden who were killed by the recent terrible explosion at Mr Ellison's tar distillery at Steanor Bottom.

The report in the *Rochdale Observer* then goes on to reproduce in full the testimony of the witnesses to the explosion and the examination and cross-examination of these witnesses. Despite evidence from the former owner of the tar distillery, John Crabtree, that he had warned Mr Ellison that morning that his still was in danger of exploding, the inquest jury found that the victims had died accidentally as a result of their excessive firing of the still.

Records show that Arthur Holt was landlord from 1893 to 1900. The *Rochdale Times* for 22 February 1896 reported that an Alfred Holt, landlord of the Summit Inn, was fined for selling rum not to standard.

In 1919, the Summit Inn Savings Club distributed £310 at the commencement of the September holidays.

LIST OF LICENSEES:

1823-1861	James Lord	1970-1983	Ernest Burt
1861	Thomas Norris	1983-1987	Vito Susca
1867-1870	John Holden	1987	Colin Ratcliffe
1870-1887	James Tetlow	1987-1995	Christopher James Court
1887-1890	Rachel Boothman	1995-1999	Donald Malcolm McClure
1890-1893	Edmund Farrar	1999	Collette Rowan
1893-1900	Arthur Holt	1999-2000	Paul Ingham
1900-1902	Arthur Farrar	2000	Nigel Dunne
1902-1914	Willie Thomas	2000	Stephen Gibley
1914-1916	James William Etchells	2000	David Walter Walker
1916-1936	Thomas Smethurst	2000	Sharon Jackson
1936-1949	John Travis Smethurst	2000-2001	Margaret Higginbotham
1949-1956	John Norris Smethurst	2001	David Etheridge
1956-1967	Ernest Cockroft Magnall	2001-2002	Anthony Paul Scarborough
1967-1968	John Dowall Greenwood	2002-2005	Marshia Baldwin
1968-1970	Norman Taylor		

Steanor Bottom and the joining of the old Turnpike Road over Calderbrook with the newer Todmorden Road along the valley floor.

Summit village.

The exposed hillside is all that remains today of Summit Brickworks, which stood to the rear of the inn.

The Summit inn sited between the main road and the Rochdale Canal.

SUN HOTEL

One of the survivors of the many pubs that used to be at this major junction of roads in the Littleborough area; this part of Littleborough is described by Edwin Waugh as, 'a flourishing little hamlet of comfortable cottages at the bottom of the brow in the high road near Stubley Hall, warmed by the "Rising Sun".'

The Sun was in existence at least as early as 1818, when James Bamford, victualler, was in residence. The house has always been a hotel, the address being, at various times, Nos 141, 100, 91, 96, Featherstall Road.

In a marriage settlement between Henry Gerard Fenton Newall and Barbara Sharp, dated 31 May 1876, mention is made of rentals valued at £700 per annum and included, 'Messuage, Mills and Lands commonly called the Featherstall Estate, comprising Public House called Sun Inn and the outbuildings and farm belonging, in the occupation of William Kay, rental £105 per annum; also Horseshoe Inn, £19 19s 0d per annum.'

This is another example of a public house where the landlord had a dual income. Sun Inn Farm existed until 1879 when on 8 March in that year a notice appeared in the *Rochdale Observer* advising an auction of livestock by instruction of William Kay (landlord) due to declining farming.

The *Rochdale Observer* reported on 6 April 1861 that a meal was served at the Sun Inn for 156 hands of Messrs Pilling, Featherstall Mill. The Sun Inn would not have been large enough to host such a large event and the meal was served at the mill. An early record of outside catering. A smaller affair was catered for on the premises in 1878 when, according to a report in the *Rochdale Observer* of 2 March that year, a tea party was held for the Lancashire & Yorkshire Productivity Society Ltd of Hare Hill Mill.

In the *Rochdale Times* for 24 November 1883 appeared the following notice:

Canary Show – On Saturday afternoon the Littleborough and Featherstall Ornithological Society, held their annual fur-feather show of canaries at the Sun Inn, Featherstall. There were 63 birds entered for the competition. The judges were Messrs Hurst and Smethurst.

The pub was rebuilt in 1910 following the passing of plans by Littleborough Urban District Council. The Littleborough Town Guide of 1968 advertised, 'Sun Hotel; 5 mins from Rochdale, Pennine Way and Hollingworth Lake.'

As with most pubs in Littleborough, efforts are regularly made to raise funds for charitable causes. An example of this was in 1980 when the Sun Inn football team played a match against the nurses of Birch Hill, raising £170 to buy a music centre for Pennine 1 Ward at Birch Hill.

LIST OF LICENSEES:

1818–1821	James Bamford	1904–1906	Fred Barker
1837	Esther Butterworth	1906–1907	John Arthur Greenwood
1843–1848	Frank Fletcher	1907–1920	Charles Smith
1851	Mary Fletcher	1920–1922	Alice Maria Smith
1852	Thomas Fletcher	1922–1931	James Butler
1858–1861	Ralph Eastham	1931–1932	John Hoare
1872–1876	Margaret Eastham	1932–1935	Thomas William Hastings
1876–1880	William Kay	1935–1954	Frank Helliwell
1880–1882	Henry Brearley	1954–1963	Bernard Flynn

The Sun Hotel on Featherstall Road.

1882–1887	John Henry Pearson	1963–1977	Clifford Blackford
1887–1893	Joseph Mather	1977–1990	Graham Rowe
1893–1895	James Haigh	1990–2005	Ann Clemenson
1895–1900	Henry Smith	2005	Lindsay Walton
1900–1904	James Fletcher		

THE TALBOT

This inn is mentioned in *Raines Manuscripts* as possibly being the Falcon Inn. The name appears in a legal document dated 20 June 1676 which was redeemable on payment of £21 4s 0d at the house of Alex Kershaw at the sign of the Talbot in Littleborough. Refer to the Falcon Inn for a fuller history and details of the licensees.

THREE HORSESHOES

This was the earlier name for the Musicians Inn on Featherstall Road. Refer to the Musicians Inn for a fuller history and details of the licensees.

TOPHAMS TAVERN

The original name for this inn was the Railway Inn. It appears to have been opened in the 1860s for we have the following mention in The Littleborough Gas Act, 1865:

Tophams Tavern, formerly
the Railway Inn.

All that Leasehold Close or Parcel of Land situate in the Hamlet or Division of Clegg in the
Township of Butterworth in the Parish of Rochdale in the County of Lancaster, belonging to the
Heirs of Richard Tattersall deceased, and whereof the said Henry Newall and Lawrence Newall are
Lessees, and which is occupied by them for the Purposes of their Gas Works, and is bounded on
the North-easterly Side by a Beerhouse also belonging to the Heirs of Richard Tattersall, whereof
Thomas Whipp is Occupier, lying between the said Land and the Road called Smithy Brow.

The inn closed in 1956, remaining closed until 1978, when it was reopened as the present
Tophams Tavern.

LIST OF LICENSEES:

1865–1869	Thomas Whipp	1910–1916	Fred Bell
1872–1874	James Brierley	1916–1920	Emily Bell
1874–1893	Jane Lord	1920–1926	Benjamin Lincoln Taylor
1893–1897	Elizabeth Tattersall	1926–1927	Charles Moran
1897–1898	Calvert Yates	1927–1945	Arthur Butterworth
1898	Hannah Harrison	1945–1956	Henry James Kirby
1898–1899	William Elliff	1956–1978	Closed
1899–1900	William Heap	1978–1985	Roland Topham
1900–1901	Willie Stott	1985–2000	Peter Madden
1901–1907	Charles Rogers	2000	Roger Achille Geirhaert
1907–1910	Lawrence Lord	2000–2005	John James Vaughan

TWO FOOT PUBLIC HOUSE

A report in the *Rochdale Observer* of 14 October 1865 of an inquest into the death of a man on
the railway gives the address of this public house as Littleborough, thus:

A Man Killed on the Railway. Last night an inquest was held at the Two Foot public-house, Littleborough, touching the death of John Barrett, aged 25 years, a cattle drover, residing at Eastwood. On the 7th Inst. the deceased took a ticket at the Littleborough station for Todmorden, by the train that leaves at 11.25 a.m., and immediately on entering the carriage he fell asleep. On the train arriving at Todmorden all the passengers with the exception of the deceased left the carriages. They were sent back empty, and when passing the Littleborough station were going at the rate of 25 miles an hour. The deceased then awoke, and finding that he was travelling in the wrong direction he jumped out of the carriage. By doing so he received such injuries that he died at half past one o'clock on Thursday. The jury returned a verdict in accordance with the above facts.

Beyond that one report, nothing has been discovered in the archives, census returns, trades directories or licensing records to indicate whether this was or was not a public house. Perhaps it was the early name for one of the public houses already mentioned in this book. We know that inquests into deaths were usually held in hostelries local to the scene of the death. This is a mystery waiting to be solved.

VICTORIA INN

The buildings in which this inn was situated were designed by architect George Mawson of Littleborough and constructed in 1869. In the 1870s the inn was owned by the Thistlethwaites. It was purchased for £900 in 1882 by John Alletson and used as security on a loan from Massey's Burnley Brewery in 1889.

Situated at the beginning of Hare Hill Road, at No. 5, the licence expired on 21 December 1910. The building eventually became Parry's shoe shop and was one of Littleborough's Leaning Buildings until it was modernised as an extension to Lincoln Jackson's hardware store, now known as Bargain Corner.

The first landlord that we have been able to find is John Alletson, who appears in the directories as a beerseller and tripe dresser. The 1881 census gives for this address:

Hare Hill Road
John Alletson; head; licensed victualler; aged 43; born Littleborough
Susannah Alletson; wife; aged 43; born Littleborough
Mary H. Alletson; daughter; barmaid, domestic; aged 20; unmarried; born Littleborough
Jane Alletson; daughter; cotton weaver; aged 18; unmarried; born Littleborough
John Alletson; son; general labourer; aged 16; unmarried; born Littleborough
William Alletson; son; scholar; aged 13; born Littleborough
James Alletson; son; scholar; aged 9; born Ratcliffe
Emma Alletson; daughter; scholar; aged 7; born Littleborough
Ethy Alletson; daughter; aged 3; born Littleborough

There is a painting in existence of a large sow that was bred by this John Alletson and commemorated in a printed handout of the 1890s, as follows:

The Last of the Giant Pig. Mr John Alletson's big pig has been so much talked about in the village, that the following account of the last end will be read with interest. It is taken from the Blackpool Herald. 'Mr Robinson, the pork butcher, did a grand stroke of business, when he secured the 'infant'

Jackson's Bargain Corner, in a former existence the Victoria Inn, situated in Littleborough's 'Leaning Buildings'.

or perhaps, to be more accurate, we should say, 'The Empress', a pretty little pig which was fed by Mr John Alletson of Littleborough and which, when alive, weighed 54 score and, when slaughtered, drew the scale at 43 score 7lbs. Considering that the animal was only 27 months old, it may be credited with having made the best use of its time. We confess we never saw such a pig before. It was well proportioned and in all respects a splendid animal. That it attracted attention will be easily understood when we say that between five and six thousand persons passed through Mr Robinson's shop on Wednesday evening. The crush was something enormous. We are informed that the weight of leaf lard taken from the animal was 50ilbs, pulling lard 25lbs, one ham 98lbs, the head 63lbs and the two kidneys, one and a third lbs.

A descendant of John Alletson, Mr Eric Alletson told the society of the time that the landlord's dog, being scented by the local pack, was mistaken for a fox. The dog ran home, closely followed by the pack, jumped through the plate glass window, closely followed by all the hounds. Objections were received against renewal of the licence in 1907 and the *Rochdale Observer* of 9 February that year reported:

> The case of the Victoria Inn, Hare Hill Road, Littleborough, was the last one heard. Mr Hodgson, barrister of Manchester, represented the owners, Massey's Burnley Brewery Company.

Inspector Purvis deposed to the house being frequented by the roughest class of people in Littleborough. The floors were unlevel, and the wall in Victoria Street seemed to be out of plumb. Within 220 yards of this house there were three fully licensed public-houses and three beerhouses.

By 1910 the inn had closed. On 17 June 1906, the *Rochdale Observer* included an advertisement which read:

> To let; four large cellars in basement, four large rooms to ground floor, large room with cooking range, three bedrooms and bathroom to first floor, hot and cold water; rent 7/6; key at Mrs Mitchell's off-licence shop, Bare Hill Street; beautify to tenants.

LIST OF LICENSEES:

1872-1904	John Alletson	1905-1910	William Fletcher
1904-1905	Thomas Clegg		

WATERSIDE INN

This was the latter name of the Railway Hotel. Refer to the Railway Hotel for a fuller history and details of the licensees.

WHEAT SHEAF HOTEL

This public house is situated in Littleborough Square, being the major part of the Roundhouse Buildings. An early reference is found in the *Stott Day Book Collection*, where mention is made that Thomas Shore, related to the Shores of Cleggswood, kept the Wheat Sheaf Inn, Littleborough, about 1780. At various times, it was known as the Sheaf Hotel and the Old Wheat Sheaf.

Travis mentions that in the 1860s, the Wheat Sheaf Inn and other old property was taken down and rebuilt further back and the inn is now a modern building with a large open space or square in front of it. These new Roundhouse Buildings were constructed in 1869, having been designed by architect James Cheetham of Rochdale.

The following record of the Littleborough Subscription Billiards Club for 1862, mentions the inn:

> That the Committee be authorised to make the best arrangement with Mr Robt. Hurst for taking the room in the Wheat Sheaf Inn for use of the club. The billiards table was bought from Burroughs Watt for £89 10s and was delivered by the L&Y Rly Co, for £1 4s 9d.

Whilst Robert Hurst was recorded as licensee for three periods in the history of this public house (1843-1866, 1866-1868, 1875-1893) he was not necessarily in occupation and managing the hotel establishment, for the 1881 census records only:

Sheaf Hotel, Church Street
Francess Whitby; head; hotel manageress; aged 33; unmarried; born Liverpool
Harriet Atherton; servant; hotel bookkeeper; aged 18; unmarried; born Liverpool
Samuel Forrest; visitor; scholar; aged 7; born Liverpool
Francis Strong; boarder; tutor; aged 26; born Bath, Lancashire
Josiah Magill; servant; waiter (formerly upholsterer); aged 60; unmarried; born Liverpool
Catherine Owen; servant; domestic servant; aged 59; widow; born Carnorvon (sic), Wales

At an auction of 1892 for the sale of the hotel, it was advertised in the following manner:

> The Hotel is a very handsome erection in the very centre of Littleborough, situated close to the railway station and is a most convenient halting place for the tourists who explore the Blackstone Edge range of hills. It is well arranged and laid out for business, is fitted with expensive furnitures, and contains Coffee Rooms, Smoke Room, Bar, six bedrooms, well fitted kitchens and is completely cellared. The

When out Shopping

call in the

Wheat Sheaf Hotel

(COMMERCIAL)

and try a

"Blue Label" Bottled Beer or Extra Stout.

Bitter and Mild Ales in sparkling condition.
"Golden Glow" Whisky a speciality.
"XXXX" an excellent nightcap.
Large Club Room available for Parties.   Bed and Breakfast.
Luncheons, Snacks, etc., at all hours.

Proprietors—

Threlfall's Brewery Co. Ltd.

Manager—Wm. McClurg.   Cook Street, Salford.

An advert for the Wheat Sheaf placed in a 1935 edition of *Littleborough Shopping Week.*

brewery adjoins the hotel and is on the modern principle. It is fitted with 30-barrel plant. It has an ample supply of water and suitable stabling.

In the same year, Mary Ellen Bradburn, was fined 1s, with 5s 6d costs for allowing her dog to roam unmuzzled.

The *Annals of Rochdale* tells us that Robert Hurst, wine and spirit merchant, aged seventy-nine, died on 23 November 1898, leaving £21,137 in his will. In 1909, the Annual Poor Children's Treat benefited by £1 17s 2d collected in the Sheaf Hotel. The 1935 shopping guide gives, 'Threlfalls Brewery, Salford, Proprietors; William McClurg, Manager; 'Blue Label' bottled stout, 'Golden Glow' whisky, 'XXXX' - an excellent nightcap.'

LIST OF LICENSEES:

1780	Thomas Shore	1935–1936	William McClurg
1818	Charles Crossley	1936–1941	Alexander Wiles Jarvis
1821	John Hirst	1941–1952	James Whitehead
1830–1831	Joseph Hartley	1952–1954	Eric Davies
1833	Mr Rowe	1954–1955	James Alexander McDonnell
1843–1866	Robert Hurst	1955	Leslie Kenneth Hayes
1866	Alice Marsden	1956–1966	Harold Saxon
1866–1868	Robert Hurst	1966–1968	Ronald Morgan
1868	David Read	1968–1969	Charles Neild
1870	Richard Gibson	1969–1973	David Deuchas Riddoch
1872–1875	David Read	1973–1974	Walter E Collinge Ridge
1875–1893	Robert Hurst	1974–1975	James Shepherd
1893–1895	John Laurence Wildgoose	1975–1976	John Charles Cooper
1895	John Mills	1976	John Cunnane
1895–1905	James Arnold	1976–1988	Kenneth Moss
1905–1912	Richard Leach Thompson	1988–1989	Norman Fred Ramsden
1912–1924	George A H Payne	1989–1990	David Marsh
1924	Jane Hannah Payne	1990–1991	Steven R Howe
1924–1930	Andrew John Kilpatrick	1991–2005	Linda Victoria Taylor
1930–1935	Joseph Henry Hammond		

WHITE HOUSE

Writing in 1857, Edwin Waugh has the following to say of the White House at the top of Blackstone Edge:

A substantial hostelrie standing prominently on the brow of the hill, called, 'The White House', and sometimes, 'Joe Faulkner's', from the name of an eccentric landlord, who kept the house in the old

The Wheat Sheaf on Littleborough Square, one of six drinking establishments within a quarter-of-a-mile of each other in the village centre.

The Wheat Sheaf photographed in 1975.

coaching time. This house can be seen from the valleys on the Lancashire side for many miles. It was a celebrated baiting-place for the great stream of travellers who went over these hills before the railway drifted it through the Vale of Todmorden.

The following extract from a poem published by 'Bill O'Jacks' emphasises this:

TH' WHITE HEAWSE

Fro' its lofty position on owd Blackstone edge
Th' White Heawse looks on th' valley below.
As tho' on th' alert like a sentinel grim,
For th' approach o' some expected foe.
But if sich be its task, –well, its useless and vain,
For th' shrill cries o' th' Moorcock, or greawse,
Are th' most frequent seawinds 'at disturb th' peaceful reign
O' silence up theer at th' White Heawse.
Ther once wur a time, tho' ere railways wur born,
When it wur no so quate as to-day;
Twur on th' main road, 'twixt Rachda' an' Halifax then
An' th' owd packhorse track passed that way.

This peace and solitude was rudely disturbed on a night at the end of the eighteenth century, as reported by the *Rochdale Observer* of 8 December 1894:

Attempted Murders on Blackstone Edge; Sensational Affair at the White House; The Landlord and Landlady Shot; A Clever Arrest; Prisoner Before the Magistrates.

A great agitation was caused in the district yesterday morning by vague news of a terrible affair which had happened in the darkness of the previous night on the top of Blackstone Edge. It was said at first that the landlord and landlady of the White House had been murdered, but fortunately this proved to be an exaggerated account of the occurrence.

The facts are these. A shabbily-dressed man entered the taproom of the White House soon after seven o'clock on Thursday night, and asked for three pennyworth of whisky. The servant, Eliza Hill, supplied the drink, and then returned to the kitchen where the landlady was sewing. When the man had been in the house about half-an-hour he began shouting for the landlord, Mr Peter McIntyre. Mrs McIntyre hurried to the taproom and told him that the landlord had gone to bed because he was unwell. At first the prisoner doubted her statement and then he asked her if she had seen his dog. When she replied that she had not he insisted on seeing the landlord. At length Mrs McIntyre went upstairs and informed her husband of what was going on. The landlord hastily dressed himself and hurried down to the tap room. The man repeated his question about his lost dog. The landlord replied that he knew nothing about it. The man then pulled out a revolver, pointed it at Mr McIntyre, and said 'Well this is it'. An exciting scene ensued. The landlady, who was standing in the doorway, screamed at the sight of the revolver, and rushed between the two men. The desperado then deliberately took aim at Mr McIntyre and fired. The bullet entered the muscle of his left arm, shattered the bone and inflicted an ugly wound. The landlady shouted for help and the man then shot at her. The bullet penetrated her bodice, glanced off the steel of her corset, and thus she escaped unhurt except for the shock. Both the landlord and landlady expected that the man intended to murder them. They ran out of the room and got behind the kitchen door and held it fast. The stranger attempted to force his way in, but failed. When they had bolted the door they climbed through the kitchen window, the servant followed them, and they concealed themselves on the

The White House, or Coach and Horses, prior to the infilling of the courtyard to extend the pub restaurant's dining capacity.

lonely moor outside. When they had been there several minutes the servant got up and went a few yards nearer the house. The assailant, who had gone round to the back of the premises, then caught sight of her white apron and stealthily crept towards her with his revolver in his hand. It was an awful moment for Mr and Mrs McIntyre, for by the dim glimmer of light through the kitchen window they could see the figure of the man approaching the girl. Eventually he caught her and said 'I will shoot your brains out if you don't tell me where they keep the money. If I don't shoot you there are three other men close by who will'. The terrified girl implored the man to have mercy, and told him that the money was kept upstairs. She then ran away across the moor, and the man returned to the house and went upstairs. He unlocked several drawers and ransacked them but he somehow missed a drawer which contained £47 and some jewellery. It would seem that the man then left the house, but no one saw him go.

In the meantime the landlady had walked across the moor in the darkness and into the main road. Her husband was in great pain and too weak from loss of blood to walk so far. The servant had fled to a farmhouse below on the Lancashire side. While Mrs McIntyre was waiting by the road a horse and trap came rapidly along. She was half afraid to stop it, for she feared that her would-be murderer and his companions were in it. When it reached her, however, she summoned up courage and shouted to the driver. He at once pulled up and then she recognised that the driver was Mr Hubert Gledhill, a coachman in the employ of Mr Samuel Heap of Littleborough. She told him in a few words of the terrible affair that had happened and then at his bidding she climbed into the trap and was driven rapidly to the Littleborough police station three miles away. No time was lost after she arrived there. Sergeant Gilbody at once telephoned to Superintendent Heywood at the Rochdale office at Townhead. The news was then flashed to the police all over the district. Nearly every police officer within a radius of six miles of Blackstone Edge was informed of what had happened and a description given of the man wanted. On both sides of the mountain a sharp lookout was kept. It was a dismal task, for the night was foggy, a cold wind blew across the moors, and rain fell nearly all the night.

The news of the occurrence spread like wildfire across the countryside, and naturally caused a great sensation. All sorts of wild rumours were afloat. In Littleborough, for instance, it was reported that a band of burglars had murdered all the occupants of the White House. Several Littleborough people walked up to the solitary inn to satisfy their curiosity. Both Dr Douglas and Dr Shield of Littleborough drove up to attend to the landlord's wound. They found Mr McIntyre in a weak and fainting condition. The humerus of the left arm was smashed, and blood was pouring profusely from the wound. They bandaged the arm and managed to extract the bullet which is almost the size of a rifle shot, and weighs about an ounce.

The capture. The story of the arrest is interesting, and shows the vigilance and prompt energy of the police. While Superintendent Heywood and Sergeant Palmer were at the White House on Thursday night a farmer in the house remarked that the birds were making 'a rare row' on the moors in the direction of Derby Bar. As soon as the superintendent returned to his office he telephoned to his sub-stations on that side of the moor, and thus caused all the men at those stations to go on to the moors on special duty. They formed a cordon along the edge of the moor on the Oldham side, and waited there until daylight. At daybreak they began to scour the moor. Soon after ten o'clock in the morning, Sergeant Ross, of Milnrow and Sergeant Davies, of Shaw, noticed a man answering to the description given walking towards Ripponden, on the road leading from Oldham to Ripponden. He was smoking a 'cutty' pipe and appeared to be quite unsuspicious. The police, however, suspected him and began to follow him at a distance. They were soon joined by two constables. At a favourable opportunity they pounced on the man and did it so suddenly that he was prevented from making any effectual resistance. He struggled to get his right hand free, but the two burly sergeants held his arms in a tight grip, while a constable searched the man's pockets. A five-chambered revolver, fully loaded, was found in the breast pocket. When charged with trying to commit murders at the White House he betrayed signs of guilt, and subsequently admitted that he committed the crime. He was then handcuffed and taken to Rochdale, where he was lodged in a cell at the Town Hall. On the way he told the police in charge of him that his name was Robert Ackrigg, and that he was a labourer hailing from Skipton. He is a mild and inoffensive looking man. Apparently he is about 28 years of age. He is 5ft 8in. high and is rather thin and pale. His complexion is dark, and his moustache and beard appeared to be of about a week's growth.

Prisoner Before The Bench; Mrs McIntyre Evidence; A Remand. The prisoner was brought up before Lieutenant Colonel Fishwick at a special sitting of the County Bench, held at the Town Hall yesterday afternoon.

Superintendent Heywood said: 'The prisoner, Robert Ackrigg, is charged with having attempted to murder Peter McIntyre, landlord of the Coach & Horses Inn, Blackstone Edge, by shooting him with a revolver; he is also charged with having attempted to murder Mrs McIntyre by shooting her with a revolver, and with having attempted to commit a felony at the house'. It appears that about a quarter to seven o'clock last night the prisoner entered the house, went into the taproom, and called for three pennyworth. He was supplied with it by Eliza Hill, the servant. At that time there was only Mrs McIntyre and the servant in the house downstairs. The prisoner remained in about a quarter of an hour, and then asked if they had a dog belonging to him. Mrs McIntyre said 'No'. He asked for the landlord, but Mr McIntyre was in bed asleep. Ultimately Mrs McIntyre went upstairs and woke her husband. He came down, and prisoner had a conversation with him about the dog. Mr McIntyre said that he had no dog belonging to the prisoner. At this time Mrs McIntyre was present, and she was about to leave the bar and go to the kitchen, when she noticed that the prisoner had a revolver, and was pointing it at her husband. She ran between them, and the prisoner immediately fired the revolver. The bullet struck her in the stomach, but fortunately the steel frame of her corset prevented the bullet penetrating her body. Of course she staggered under the shock. Prisoner then fired at Mr McIntyre. He raised his left arm, and the bullet struck him on the arm and penetrated three or four inches. Mrs McIntyre then got out of the bar into the kitchen, and she and the servant held the door against the prisoner. Prisoner called out that if they didn't open the door he would shoot them. They did not open it and prisoner kept the door pressed to. After a while he went away, and Mr and Mrs McIntyre and the servant ultimately got through the kitchen window on to some vacant land behind the house. Shortly afterwards the prisoner went to the back of the house, and saw the servant, presented the revolver at her and told her that if she didn't tell him where the money was he would shoot her. She said it was upstairs. Prisoner then left her, and nothing more was seen of him till ten o'clock this morning, when Sergeant Ross, of Milnrow, and Sergeant Davis, of Shaw, saw him in Rishworth, in Yorkshire, about a mile from the Tup Inn public-house. They suspected him to be the man they wanted, seized him, and found in his pocket a loaded revolver with five chambers (the revolver was here produced.) Each chamber was loaded. The officers found five other cartridges in the prisoner's possession. They took him into custody, and charged him with having attempted to murder both Mr and Mrs McIntyre, and he said, 'its right; I'll make no resistance'. After the affair at the White House medical aid was called to Mr McIntyre and after a long search Dr Douglas and Dr Shields, of Littleborough, with the assistance of Dr MacGill, found the bullet embedded between the broken ends of the bone of Mr McIntyre's left arm. The bullet that had entered Mrs McIntyre's clothes was found on the floor of the kitchen. I am not prepared (said Superintendent Heywood) to go on with the case to-day, as Mr McIntyre is confined to bed: and I shall only offer sufficient evidence for a remand for a week. The prisoner has been placed with a number of other men this afternoon and both Mrs McIntyre and her servant have identified him as the man who shot her. I call Mrs McIntyre.

Mrs McIntyre. Ellen McIntyre said: I am the wife of Peter McIntyre, who is the landlord of the Coach & Horses Inn, Blackstone Edge. About seven o'clock last night I saw the prisoner in the taproom, and had some conversation, with him. When I first saw him I was in the kitchen, and he called out to me. I could not say whether he asked for me or for the master first, but he did ask for the master, and I told him that he could not see the master just then. 'Will he be long?' he said, and I went into the bar and told him my husband was in bed. 'But I have come about a dog,' he said, adding that he had heard that morning from Shackleton that it was at our house, and that we had it 'made up'. I said we had no dog, and had not seen any strange dogs. Prisoner was not satisfied: he wanted to see Peter. 'Is he ill?' he asked, and I told him my husband was not particularly bad. Prisoner said he wanted him 'to write him a letter or two'. So I went into the kitchen and got a candle. I said to the girl, 'I expect he thinks Peter is not at home.' Prisoner did not hear that. I went upstairs and woke Peter, and he came downstairs. When I had got back to the bar, prisoner was in the taproom. Peter asked what he was wanted for, and I told him what prisoner had said about the dog. He said he knew nothing about the dog, and prisoner told him he wanted him to write a line or two. Peter said he wouldn't do any such thing. Prisoner walked away and I followed him out of the taproom. 'Perhaps he wanted to know whether we have a dog,' I said, and immediately prisoner presented a revolver at my husband, and then he shot me. I didn't see the shot which struck my husband and I don't know which of us he shot first.

Lieutenant-Colonel Fishwick: That is sufficient, I think, except for identification. Mrs McIntyre: I am sure he is the same man. I have identified him from among many other men, some of whom I knew.

The Magistrate's Clerk: Is your husband in bed? – Yes.

Asked if he had any questions to put to the witness, prisoner appeared to make no reply, but the officer in the dock with him said he had answered 'No.'

The Arrest. Police-sergeant Ross, of Milnrow, said that at about ten o'clock that morning, he, in company with Police-sergeant Davis, of Shaw, apprehended the prisoner at Higher Bridge, Booth Dean, Yorkshire. They saw him coming along the road for about fifty yards. When he got close to them he glanced round, and from the description they had received they recognised that he was the man wanted. Davis snared him by the arms. Prisoner was very reluctant to take his right hand out of his pocket, but they pulled it out and found that he had a revolver in his trousers' pocket. It was fully loaded. Witness then charged him with the attempted double murder of the landlord and landlady of the White House. He replied, 'It's right: I'll make no resistance.' We then brought him to Rochdale.

Superintendent Heywood then asked that the prisoner might be remanded to the cells. Lieutenant-Colonel Fishwick said the prisoner will be remanded till three o'clock next Friday afternoon. The prisoner was then removed from the dock.

We find in the *Annals of Rochdale* that he was sentenced to twelve years penal servitude on 23 February 1895.

On 24 October 1857 the *Rochdale Times* reported that the landlord, William Oldfield, had been fined ten shillings following a summons for serving drink on a Sunday. The census for 1881 finds at the White House:

> *Blackstone Edge Top*
> Ellen Brearley; head; licensed victualler; age 24; widow; born Littleborough
> Sarah Hill; sister; general servant; age 15; born Littleborough
> William Hill; brother; fulling miller; age 20; unmarried; born Littleborough

The *Rochdale Observer* in 1896 reported in a round up of the year's news that the sudden death of the landlord, Peter McIntyre, had occurred on 23 October that year. What is of further interest is that the jury for the inquest objected to the coroner at having to attend inquests at the inn. The common occurrence of coroner's inquests being held in local hostelries was perhaps not objectionable to juries until one is held in a public house that is remote from the town and not particularly accessible without transportation.

LIST OF LICENSEES:

1840	Joe Faulkner	1919–1920	George Henry Riley
1843	Harriet Faulkner	1920–1924	Larnia Matilda Hughes
1851–1857	William Oldfield	1939–1960	Frank Cropper
1861–1879	Abraham Spencer	1960–1961	Annie Cropper
1879–1880	Edmund Brierley	1961–1963	Robert Gordon G Stevenson
1880–1881	Ellen Brearley	1963–1967	Stanley Smith
1881–1896	Peter McIntyre	1967–1971	Arthur Booth
1896–1897	Ellen McIntyre	1971–1976	Raymond Jackson
1897–1901	Adam Hill	1976–1983	Walter Frederick Bracegirdle
1901–1906	Fred Hirst	1983–1984	James R Sutton
1906–1911	James Palmer	1984–1990	Neville Marney
1912–1917	James Parker	1990–2005	Richard Neville Marney
1917–1919	William Crabtree		

WOODCOCK

This inn was in the valley between the A58 and Sladen Fold, know locally as The Gap. The area is mentioned in the early records as Watergate. Referring again to Travis' *Notes on Littleborough*, we find the following reference to 'Old Tom of Water Yate':

> While in this quarter, we should not forget to mention one old and familiar personage – 'Old Tom of Water Yate' – who at a later date kept a beerhouse just below the main road and in the days when wedding

A modern view of the White House frontage and the in-filled courtyard.

The rear of the public house, with Littleborough just visible on the valley floor below.

The Pennine Way panorama with the White House in the centre.

parties from Todmorden and Walsden had to go to the Parish Church, Rochdale, to have the nuptial knot tied or pay extra fees at their own church, the family made good substantial dinners and teas for visitors at reasonable charges, so that after a walk of seven or eight miles to get wed before morning service, then a short rest at some pub in town, and a walk back again to Water Yate, people were quite ready for 'Old Tom's' provisions, which were sure to be ample and ready for them any Sunday of the year.

The following reference in the 1851 census gives a few more details about the Eddas family:

Watergate
Thomas Eddas; 77 (head); victualler
Edmund Eddas; 36 (son); fuller
Rebecca Eddas; 27 (daughter); general servant
John Dixon; lodger; labourer

The 1881 census records:

Woodcock Inn, Sladen Mill
Thomas Stott; head; fulling miller and farmer of 3 acres; aged 55; born Littleborough
Rebecca Stott; wife; aged 56; born Littleborough
Maria Stott; daughter; servant; aged 23; unmarried; born Littleborough

The following extract from a letter sent to the society by a Nora Colclough, whose family had the pub in the 1930s, gives an interesting insight into the age of the building that was demolished in the 1940s:

Her father, Noah Colclough, was licensed from the late 1920s to the 1930s. During the time that she lived at the Woodcock, a chimney beam became ignited and caused a fire. A dog, a whippet, that her father had purchased from some tinkers, because it was in a very neglected condition, saved the family's lives by barking and awakening them during the early hours of Sunday morning. During rebuilding, churchwardens' pipes were found in the cavity of the wall. The wall plaster was mixed with hair as was the custom at the time that the Woodcock was built.

The *Rochdale Times* on 11 April 1908 reports that the landlord was Merrick Howarth and was discharged from bankruptcy. Records show that his wife, Hannah, was the licensee.

LIST OF LICENSEES:

1845–1852	Thomas Eddas	1913–1923	Frank Oswald Partington
1861–1883	Thomas Stott	1923–1924	Fred Whittaker
1883–1884	Rebecca Stott	1924–1925	Thomas Dugdale
1884	Ann Brearley	1925–1926	Henry Hodgkinson
1884–1899	Richard Rigg	1926–1937	Noah Colclough
1899–1900	Helliwell Rigg	1937–1938	Joseph Halmett
1900–1906	Merrick Howarth	1938–1940	John Walker
1906–1911	Hannah Howarth	1940–1941	Robert Osborne
1911–1912	John Edward Cross	1941–1942	Vera Mary Osborne
1912–1913	John Heywood		

The Woodcock in
Sladen Fold.

A snow-bound
Woodcock Inn.

The site of the
Woodcock Inn at
Sladen Fold.

APPENDICES

WHERE ARE THEY NOW?

Below are a list of the public houses, inns, hotels, beerhouses and ale houses that records show as having existed in Littleborough. Where no longer trading, we have listed the known date of closure and the current use of the property.

Name	Closed	Current property use (where no longer licensed)
Bay Mare	1915	Off licence, Church Street
Beach Hotel; Millers		
Black Sloven; Hare & Hounds	1869	Ruin; undergoing renovation as private dwelling
Blue Ball	1964	Demolished; adjacent site of the Smithy Bridge
Blue Bell	1958	Demolished; site of Crowther Court, Dearnley
Butchers; Bull & Butchers	1820	Property dismantled/re-erected at Summit Inn
Caldermoor; Dog & Partridge		
Church Tavern	1861	Possible forerunner of the Horseshoe, Church St.
Duke of York	1843	Converted to private dwelling; Ealees
Dyers Arms		
Falcon Inn; The Talbot		
Fisherman's Inn	2004	Now the Wine Press bistro
Friendly Arms	?	Location not yet identified
Gale Inn	1990s	Now the New China Palace restaurant
Golden Fleece	1880	Church Street, property not yet identified
Hare & Hounds	?	Location in Dearnley not yet identified
Horseshoe (Featherstall)	1909	Demolished; junction Whittle St/Featherstall Road
Horseshoe (Littleborough)	1917	Converted to Littleborough Trades Hall, Church St.
Huntsman; Royal Oak		
King William IV		
Lake Hotel	1939	Demolished
Lancashire & Yorkshire Hotel	1911	Demolished; site of private dwellings, Lake Bank
Lodge Inn	1917	Converted to private dwellings; Rakewood Road
Lydgate Inn; Gate Inn	1980s	Converted to private dwelling; Blackstone Edge
Mermaid Inn	1911	Demolished in 1940s
Miners Arms	?	Converted to private dwelling; Ealees
Moorcock		
Musicians Arms	1935	Converted to private dwelling; Calderbrook
Musicians Inn; Three Horseshoes	1907	Converted to private dwelling; Featherstall Road
New Inn; Colliers Arms		

Ox and Plough		
Parkhill House	1942	Converted to private dwelling; Shore
Punchbowl Inn	1908	Converted to private dwellings; Summit
Queen Anne; Queen's Head	1934	Converted to private dwelling; Handle Hall
Queen's Hotel (Hollingworth Lake)	1923	Converted to private dwelling; Hollingworth Lake
Queen's Hotel (Littleborough)		
Railway Inn/Hotel; Waterside	2003	Converted to Waterside restaurant
Rake Inn; Hayrake		
Red Lion		
Rock Tavern	1915	Converted to private dwelling; Rock Nook
Royal Exchange		
Royal Oak (Littleborough)		
Royal Oak (Smithy Bridge)	1924	Demolished; site of nursing home, Smithy Bridge
Seven Stars (Schofield Hall)	1832	Ruin
Shepherds Tavern; Shepherds Rest	1915	Converted to private dwellings; Blackstone Edge
Sloop Inn, Durn	1843	Location not yet identified
Smithy Bridge; New Blue Ball		
Sportsmans; Dog & Partridge		
Star Hotel	1942	Converted to private dwelling; Hollingworth Lake
Stubley Hall	1999	Converted to private dwelling; Featherstall Road
Summit Inn		
Sun Hotel		
Tophams Tavern; Railway Inn		
Two Foot Public House	?	Location not yet identified
Victoria Inn	1910	Hardware Shop, Hare Hill Road
Wheat Sheaf Hotel		
White House; Coach & Horses		
Woodcock	1942	Demolished; Sladen Fold

APPENDIX II

NOTES ON STUBLEY

The following extract is taken from the *Transactions of Lancashire & Cheshire Antiquarian Society*, Volume 21, 1903, Pp 202-3:

Stubley, with its neighbourhood, was always noted for good ale. From its situation, exposed to all the rigors of that hilly region, the climate was reckoned so cold as to require that their daily beverage should be of sufficient strength to counteract its effect. That the habits of intemperance could be contracted from the constant use of such stimulants may be easily inferred. The following letter from Nicholas Stratford, Bishop of Chester, to James Holt of Castleton [Rochdale], is but too melancholy a confirmation of the inference:

"*Sir, - your request, on behalf of Mr Helliwell, was easily granted: for I am myself inclined to give the best encouragement I can to the poor curates, as long as they continue diligent in the discharge of their duty. But I have now, sir, a request to make to you, which I heartily pray you may as readily grant me; and that is that you will, for the future, abandon and abhor the sottish vice of drunkenness, which (if common fame be not a great liar) you are much addicted to. I beseech you, sir, frequently and seriously to consider that many dismal fruits and consequences of this sin, even in this world – how destructive it is to all your most valuable concerns and interests; how it blasts your reputation, destroys your health, and will (if continued) bring you to a speedy and untimely death; and which is infinitely more dreadful, will exclude you from the Kingdom of Heaven, and expose you to that everlasting fire where you will not be able to obtain so much as one drop of water to cool your tongue….I assure you, sir, this advice now given you proceeds from sincere love and the earnest desire to promote your happiness, both in this world, and in the next, and I hope you will be pleased so to accept from your affectionate friend and humble servant."*

N. Cestriens, Chester
November 1699

APPENDIX III

LOCAL PUB SPORTS

This page consists of a few notes on some of the older sports that are no longer played. They are not necessarily pub games but have always been associated with pubs and those that frequent them.

Knurr and Spell
The following consists of hitting a small projectile over as long a distance as possible and was played locally up to about 1930. Harold Tate, Parkhill House, remembers playing this in the field behind the Royal Oak in Smithy Bridge; Mabel Luke, mother to Alan Luke, remembered it being played in Bobby's Field at Gatehouse.

Variations of the same were 'Spring Knurr' and 'Peggy'. It was described on the BBCs *University Challenge* as 'Poor Man's Golf'. An article in the *Rochdale Observer* of 13 June 1931 describes the game as follows:

By the sudden and immediate release of a spring, the projectile is thrown forwards and upwards to a convenient height, according to its regulations, for the striker to hit and drive forward. The 'knurr', which is made of pot (used to be wood), is placed in a cup which is at the end of a long flat spring – probably the 'spell' proper owing to the original being formed from a spell of wood. The spring is bent backwards and held in position by a pawl … the player … taps the pawl, this releases the spring which throws the ball upwards and forwards in the air, whilst with a wide-sweeping stroke the player does his best to hit the ball and make the longest drive possible.

Pitch and Toss
This was played as pure gambling with two coins, betting on odds and evens. The game was illegal, with young boys often earning a few pennies by staying on lookout, in case the police came. The following extract from the *Rochdale Observer* of 15 March 1866 has local connections, 'Gambling William Greenwood and George Holt were charged by the police with playing Pitch & Toss on Sunday last, near Hollingworth. They were dismissed on payment of costs. John Shaw and Henry Buckley were charged with a similar offence and dismissed in the same way.'

Quoits
This game involved throwing heavy iron rings over a peg set in a clay box. Two boxes being the 'ends', some thirty yards apart and, apparently, varying sizes of rings were used. These were shown to the original author by Harold Tate.

Similar games were played inside pubs, with bullrings, being variations on hoop-la. At the Bird i'th' Hand at Walsden, there was a hook on the wall with a ring hanging from the roof a short distance in front. The string was just long enough to land the ring on the hook. It was, apparently, difficult for players unused to the technique, to land the ring in place. The landlady was, however, very adept at the game.

APPENDIX IV

ASSIZES AND LICENSING

The following notes have been extracted from Volumes 58 & 59 of the *Transactions of Lancashire & Cheshire Antiquarian Society*:

Control over the quality of bread and ale was also linked with the regulation of their prices. Whilst the price of corn was left to haggling in the market, charges for bread and ale were governed by a sliding scale known as the Assizes of Bread & Ale. These date from at least the thirteenth-century and were first imposed by Royal Ordinances and later by legislation. The Assize that was believed to have been formulated in 1266 regulated the price of ale to the cost of barle'y.

The following appears in the Magna Carta, 'Let there be throughout the Kingdom a single measure for wine, a single measure for ale and a single measure for corn, namely, 'The London Quarter.'

The Assize of 1266 provided that when barley stood at two shillings a quarter, four gallons of ale should be sold for one penny and for each successive rise of six pence in the price of barley, the number of gallons for a penny should drop by half. Afterwards, other scales were promulgated by the central government of the day, reflecting in the increase in the price of ale, the continuing diminution in the value of money, with probable local variations.

In mediaeval times, there was no legislative interference with the freedom of individuals to sell ale or keep an alehouse, but towards the end of the fifteenth-century the growth of crime and disorder associated with drinking made some form of state control necessary. The end of the Civil War and the break up of the armies of feudal retainers, set loose hordes of riotous men who flocked to the towns, where they kept themselves by theft and violence and spent their ill-gotten gains on dicing and consuming potions in public houses. To check this evil, an act against vagabonds and unlawful games was passed in 1494, empowering the Justices of the Peace to 'put away common ale selling in towns and places where they should think convenient and to take sureties of the keepers of alehouses in their good behaviour'.

From this beginning developed the English licensing system.

In 1552, it was enacted that no-one should be allowed to keep a common alehouse or 'tippling house' without obtaining the permission of two or more Justices and entering into suitable sureties.

The early part of the seventeenth-century saw the experiences of the local justices in attaching suitable conditions on license holders in line with acts of Parliament. These conditions included the compulsory use of standard measures, no ale selling during divine services etc. (The weights and measures of the town of Rochdale 'kept by ye Marketlooker', were stated to belong to Lord Byron).

The well-known obligation of innkeepers to provide lodging, is exemplified by the order in Burnley of 1498 that insisted that 'no man nor woman should brew ale to sell but that they luge both man and horse ably'.

An ordinance for Manchester innkeepers of 1556 required that 'they make two honest beddes and every one of them shall put furthe of his windoe or some other convenient place a syne of a hand pentid', larger inns being allowed to put out whatever signs they wished.

By 1729, the Brewster Sessions were the organ of control over licensing and in 1830 the Beerhouse Act was introduced to 'cater for the growing urban population and to keep the working man away from the evils of the sin house'. The new law allowed any householder, fulfilling certain conditions, to turn his house into a 'beer-shop'. This is best illustrated by this note on 'Tom & Jerry Shops' which appeared in a small booklet entitled, *A Look at the Past*:

> Many of the cottagers brewed their own beer and would lend each other a pint or a quart of this beverage. On the 10 October 1828, a law was passed granting to cottagers a license to sell ale or porter to be consumed off the premises. Four cottages were at once converted into what was known as Tom & Jerry Shops and did good business, for they were able to sell liquor cheaper than the publicans on account of being under less rent. Customers would knock at the windows of these 'Jerry Shops' would tender their money and the beer or porter was handed through and consumed on the street. In October 1830, the law was further altered, giving beersellers' customers the privilege of consuming beer on the premises. This amendment to the law caused the number of beersellers to increase to above a score in the town.

The Licensing Act of 1872 was the first to give powers to the local authorities to grant licenses, this being done previously by Customs & Excise. It is these records of the local authority that are now kept at the magistrates court. This Act stopped the increase in the number of beerhouses during the latter half of the nineteenth-century. It was not until the Compensation Act of 1904 that significant closures began to be made. By this act, local authorities were required to compensate the owners and tenants of pubs if they felt that the pubs should be closed because the premises were thought to be undesirable or in need of redevelopment.

From Volume 20 of the transactions, we have the following note on beer:

> The art of malting and the use of beer are supposed to have been introduced into Britain by the Romans. Beer and vinegar were the ordinary beverage of the soldiers under Julius Caesar. Beer being so suitable to the climate and so easily made by an agricultural people with plenty of corn, soon became the national beverage. Previous to this the usual drinks of the Ancient Britons were water, milk and mead, (an intoxicating drink made from honey). According to the 'Alvismal', a Scandinavian poem of the 10th Century it is called ale among men and among the Gods, beer.

The Penguin edition of *History of Science & Technology* tells us that:

> By the tenth century, hops came to the fore; monasteries were starting to grow hops and the slightly bitter-hopped beer began to compete fiercely with the older 'fruit beer' and other types of spiced beer and unspiced malted beverages which were then called 'Ale'. By the end of the fifteenth century, this long struggle was finally decided by the victory of hopped beer.

APPENDIX V

BREWERY FAMILY TREES

This series of trees is intended to show how the local inns have become part of the major brewing companies of the age. The dates indicate the date in which each particular brewery was taken over or merged with the company above it and the dates with the pubs indicate when it was bought by the company above them. There are some uncertainties, but we have tried to be as accurate as possible, by referring to licensing records and books such as, *Where have all the Breweries Gone?* by Norman Barber.